Saratoga Tales

Saratoga Tales

*Great Horses, Fearless Jockeys, Shocking
Upsets and Incredible Blunders at
America's Legendary Race Track*

Bill Heller

Whitston Publishing Company, Inc.
Albany, New York
2004

To Tom Gilcoyne & Virginia O'Brien

Tom Gilcoyne,
the Historian of the National Museum of Racing and Hall of Fame
&
Virginia O'Brien,
the Director of the Saratoga Harness Hall of Fame, who
have spent much of their lives doing everything they can to
promote horse racing in Saratoga Springs.

Other books by Bill Heller

Obsession: Bill Musselman's Relentless Quest

Overlay, Overlay

The Will To Win: The Ron Turcotte Story

Playing Tall: The Ten Shortest Players in NBA History

Harness Overlays

Travelin' Sam—America's Sports Ambassador

Exotic Overlays

Billy Haughton—The Master

Turf Overlays

Thoroughbred Legends: Go for Wand

Thoroughbred Legends: Forego

Thoroughbred Legends: Personal Ensign

Graveyard of Champions

Run Baby Run

A Good Day Has No Rain

Go For the Green

Contents

Acknowledgements ix

<u>Chapter</u>
1   Only in Saratoga 1

2   They Bet the Wrong Horse 7

3   Last Dance...25

4   Left Behind..37

5   Angel..55

6   Dave 73

7   Oops...91

8   Lightning Strikes...................................109

9   Fall from Grace......................................115

10   California Dreamers 121

11   The End of the World 134

12   Nose Jobs...143

13   Thirty-Six and Counting 149

14   An Unfunny Travers 157

15   Another Four Bite the Dust 169

My Own Saratoga Tale 179

Index 185

Acknowledgments

This is my 17th book, yet I am still amazed by the incredible number of people who offer to do anything they can to help you along the way, even if you're a complete stranger.

My 15-year-old son Benjamin, is no stranger, and he was an incredible asset: getting information, checking information, listening to the entire manuscript and offering useful suggestions. He was also tolerant of his dad disappearing into the den many nights.

Tom Gilcoyne, the retiring historian of the National Museum of Racing and Hall of Fame; his able replacement Alan Carter, and my good friend Dick Hamilton were a huge help. Alan and Tom did an extraordinary job of sifting through old charts to assist my research. I am deeply indebted.

The entire staff of the Keeneland Library, one of the great treasures of the racing industry, were, as always, incredibly helpful. Thanks to Cathy Schenk, Phyllis Rogers and Laura White.

My buddy, Joan Lawrence, and Bonnie Cooper of the National Thoroughbred Racing Association provided endless data to me on horses, jockeys and trainers.

My friends at the New York Racing Association, Glen Mathes, Fran LaBelle, Charlotte Quinn, the multi-talented Jason Blewitt and Barry Schwartz, who convinced me to include a chapter on Affirmed-Alydar's Travers, were a huge help. Photographer Adam Coglianese, too.

My friend, Tom Conoby, and his son, Darren, let me borrow their entire collection of Secretariat artifacts. Tom also shared his memories from Secretariat's Sanford Stakes victory. The genesis of that chapter came from another friend, Mark Cusano, who co-hosts a great weekly OTB cable-TV show and may be the best handicapper on the planet. Another friend and astute handicapper, Bob Gersowitz, offered his memories from the Sanford. That chapter could not have been done without the assistance of Jean Root Mahalov of the College of Saint Rose's Neil Hellman Library. Linda's Chief's retired trainer Al Scotti was a great help and a great interview, and Neil Hellman's wife, Edith, daughter Joyce and son-in-law Sanford Bookstein shared their stories, scrapbooks and their house with a writer they had never met. I thank them sincerely. My good friend Howard Nolan shared his memories of his friend, Neil, too. Thanks, Howard.

Bonnie von Wiesenthal was a treasure, allowing Benjamin and I to visit her at her Snowberry Farm and share her scrapbooks. She then gave us a personal tour.

Karen Johnson of the Daily Racing Form helped me research the chapter about her amazing dad, trainer Phil Johnson, who has won at least one race at Saratoga for the past 36 years.

Jim Murello shared his moving film about Fourstardave, which was a great source of information.

Joe and Sean Clancy helped a ton in the chapter about Sean's eventful ride on Roberto's Grace at Saratoga.

Marshall Cassidy went out of his way to run down family members for the chapter about his uncle, George.

Thanks to Bob Curran of the Jockey Club; Eric South of the Jockey Guild; Jane DeCoteau of the New York Thoroughbred Breeders, Inc.; Stacy Clifford of the New York State Racing and Wagering Board; Norma Vermeer, Stu Zanville, Jane Goldstein and Bob Benoit.

Angel Cordero, Jerry Bailey, Ron Turcotte, Chris McCarron, Braulio Baeza, John Veitch, Patrice Wolfson, Richard Bomze, Richard Migliore, Leo O'Brien, Keith O'Brien, Lucas Dupps, Tom Skiffington, Jr., Brian Cassidy, Frank Lovato, Jr., John Pricci, Jose Santos, Ruben Hernandez, Chip

Miller, Wally Dollase, Don Orlando, Jim Bond, Jack Knowlton, Frank Coppola, Jr., John Velazquez, Todd Pletcher, Allen Jerkens and Phil Johnson all found the time to do interviews.

The *Daily Gazette* was a tremendous help with photographs and I thank Jack Hume, Tom Woodman, Susan Whiteman, Cecil Walker and David Krause.

Thanks to Ed Lewi, Mark Bardack and Cate Masterson of Ed Lewi Associates.

Barb Livingston didn't let the Kentucky Derby prevent her from contributing her magnificent photos. Thanks, Barb.

To anyone I missed, I apologize.

Finally, I thank my dog Belle Mont for not eating the manuscript.

The SARATOGIAN

3 left at the gate in a racing rarity

LEFT AT THE GATE—Move It Now is left behind at the gate in the 8th race at Saratoga racetrack Wednesday.
(Photo by Clark Bell, Courtesy of The Saratogian)

CHAPTER 1

Only in Saratoga

"If it can happen, it happens at Saratoga," 74-year-old George Cassidy, the long-time starter for the New York Racing Association, said, August 8, 1980.

He knew better than anyone. The day before at historic Saratoga Race Course, Cassidy, who followed his father into the profession and started horses for 51 years at Saratoga, Belmont Park, Aqueduct Racetrack and Jamaica, had made the second mistake of an otherwise distinguished career spanning some 125,000 races. With the filly Move It Now, the final horse in the 1980 Dewitt Clinton Stakes, about to enter her outside stall in the starting gate, Cassidy pressed the button, sending most, but not all, of the horses on their way. Move It Now's jockey, Ruben Hernandez, looked stunned behind the starting gate. Everybody was stunned, Cassidy included.

"The last—and only—mistake I made was right here at Saratoga 24 years ago," he told Tom Cunningham, the sports editor of the Albany *Times Union*, the next day. "I had a horse behind a van which carried officials to the starting gate. I sent the field away without him."

To his considerable credit, Cassidy took complete responsibility for his second mistake, which triggered an unprecedented series of events, including the re-running of the stakes race without Move It Now, who was injured in the interim.

Saratoga Race Course has been saturated with unprecedented events ever since its unlikely opening in the middle of
the Civil War, August 3, 1863. Saratoga's unique Victorian
charm and hallowed traditions have been attracting racing
fans to Saratoga Springs every summer for 14 decades. In
1999, *Sports Illustrated* named Saratoga Race Course as "one of
the Top Ten sporting venues in the world." Two years later,
ESPN Magazine called Saratoga "the loveliest racetrack in the
country." Nobody, perhaps, said it better than the brilliant
sports columnist Red Smith, who once offered directions to
Saratoga Race Course in a column: "From New York City, you
drive north for about 175 miles, turn left on Union Avenue and
go back 100 years."

From the misty mornings on the backstretch, through
workouts staged before visitors breakfasting on luscious hand
melons in the clubhouse, past the stark drama of the country's
best Thoroughbreds and jockeys battling nine times in the
afternoon, to the parties that last well into the next day,
Saratoga is a unique, short-lived experience lasting just six
weeks every summer. That is why hundreds, if not thousands,
of New York State workers in nearby Albany plan their vaca-
tions to coincide with the meet. It is the reason tourists come
from all over to attend the Yearling Sales or the inductions at
the National Museum of Racing and Hall of Farm or the annual Jockey Club Round Table Conference or a myriad of other
events tied to the meet.

When the New York Racing Association holds its annual Open House on the Sunday before the meet begins that
Wednesday, crowds range upwards of 15,000. They come to
watch bet-less races, sit in clubhouse boxes, take backstretch
tours and enjoy the carnival like atmosphere. Other tracks
would kill to get 15,000 people for a day of real racing.

If there is one tradition which embodies Saratoga, it is
the shocking upsets in major stakes races there perpetrated on
many of the greatest Thoroughbreds to ever step onto a racetrack. Ask racing fans to name the greatest two horses of the
20th Century, and more times than not, you'll hear the names

of Secretariat and Man o' War in either order. Though they raced more than 50 years apart, they are forever linked by their historic losses at Saratoga Race Course, where Man o' War suffered his only defeat in the 1919 Sanford Stakes to a horse named Upset, and the site of Secretariat's shocking loss to Onion in the 1973 Whitney Handicap.

That is why Saratoga is forever known as the "Graveyard of Champions." But at least Man o' War and Secretariat made it into the starting gate on the afternoon of their unexpected defeats in stakes races. Move It Now did not on that strange afternoon in 1980.

And Move It Now had a kinder fate than the filly Allumeuse, who was the victim of an even more infamous race at Saratoga six years later, when three stewards disqualified the wrong horse, her, then made it official before learning of their mistake. The Allumeuse Affair, as it became known, left bettors with legitimate winning tickets still worthless to this very day, while allowing the luckiest bettors in the history of horse racing to cash losing tickets, lots of losing tickets. And Allumeuse, much like Move It Now, was never the same, suffering a tragic ending soon afterwards.

On an August afternoon nine years after Allumeuse's disqualification, a horse named Roberto's Grace seemed on the way to winning a steeplechase race at Saratoga easily when his saddle slipped. Jockey Sean Clancy desperately tried to hold onto his horse's neck until the finish line, but did not quite make it. Or at least it looked like he did not make it. The same photo finish which would determine the results of a desperately close finish between Roberto's Grace and Big Band Show would also reveal if Clancy had held on to the finish line. If he had not, Roberto's Grace would have been disqualified for not carrying his weight the entire distance of the race. Clancy's souvenir from the incident was a concussion, which has not interfered with his burgeoning success as a writer.

A year before he was upset in the 1973 Whitney, Secretariat posted his own upset in the Sanford Stakes over previously undefeated Linda's Chief, owned by Albany theater owner/philanthropist Neil Hellman. Linda's Chief was the only horse favored over Secretariat in his 21 lifetime starts and, despite meeting an untimely end, would leave a lasting legacy of his owner's immense generosity.

Nine years before Funny Cide made celebrities of his Saratoga-based owners in 2003 by becoming the first New York-bred to win the Kentucky Derby and Preakness Stakes, another New York-bred, Fourstardave, won a race at Saratoga for the eighth consecutive year. The feat was so remarkable that a street and a Saratoga stakes race were re-named in his honor. A Fourstardave Award is now given annually for special achievement at Saratoga.

But there are even longer Saratoga streaks. Hall of Fame jockey Angel Cordero won 11 consecutive Saratoga riding titles from the 1970s through the 1980s, while Hall of Fame trainer Phil "P. G." Johnson has won at least one race at Saratoga for 36 consecutive years.

Every summer, poignant stories spring from Saratoga Race Course. One of the most memorable runnings of Saratoga's marquee race, the $1 million Travers Stakes, was a confluence of four battles in 1997:

- A wicked, hail-producing thunderstorm challenging an ingenious track superintendent 24 hours before the race.
- California Hall of Fame jockey Chris McCarron, whose mother had just passed away and was unsure if he would even show up for the Travers, vs. New York Hall of Fame jockey Jerry Bailey, who has been dominating Saratoga for years.
- Unheralded New York trainer Jim Bond seeking his second consecutive Travers victory vs. California trainer Wally Dollase, who had visited Saratoga frequently, but never even started a horse at Saratoga Race Course, let alone one in the Travers.

- Finally, two horses who staged a stretch-
  long battle of will right to the finish line,
  Bond and Bailey's Behrens vs. Dollase
  and McCarron's Deputy Commander.

"It's the most exciting thing in racing, to come down the stretch with two powerful horses and two good jockeys," McCarron, who retired and is now Santa Anita's General Manager, said in 2003. "There's no feeling like that."

Saratoga fans got that feeling twice within an hour on an afternoon in 2002, two stakes races in the same day decided by inches, both races too close to tell who had won.

Two years earlier, there were two, and darn near three winners of a single stakes race, the prestigious Hopeful, run in a terrifying backdrop of a vicious, thunderstorm producing terrifying bolts of lightning just as those inexperienced two-year-olds headed onto the track. Such thunderstorms are commonplace at Saratoga. An even worse storm had previously forced the New York Racing Association to cancel part of a racing program for the first time ever. Then it happened again.

Other Saratoga memories are more frivolous: an obviously irrational scribe—one of many—foolishly tempting fate by riding a horse out of the starting gate at Saratoga even though he did not know how to ride a horse. All for a T-shirt.

There are dozens of Thoroughbred tales from Saratoga. Here are a few.

Linda's Chief winning the Saranac, Braulio Baeza up.
(*Photo Courtesy of Joyce Hellman Bookstein*)

The Saranac Presentation.
In the winner's circle are, left to right:
trainer Al Scotti, Neil Hellman, jockey Braulio Baeza,
actor Telly Savalas and Neil's wife, Edith.
(*Photo Courtesy of Joyce Hellman Bookstein*)

CHAPTER 2

They Bet the Wrong Horse

There was a buzz in the paddock before the featured Sanford Stakes at Saratoga Race Course, August 16, 1972. Undefeated Linda's Chief, named by Albany theater owner Neil Hellman for his granddaughter, was the focus of most people's attention.

Back then, horses were saddled individually around one of the majestic elms in Saratoga's unfenced, expansive paddock. A cardboard number matching each horse's program number was affixed to a single tree. The more popular the Thoroughbred, the bigger the ring of people watching him get saddled.

"I went back to look at the horses and there was an enormous crowd around Linda's Chief, about five deep," Bob Gersowitz, now a 50-year-old attorney for New York State, said. "You couldn't get close to him."

Rival two-year-olds hadn't gotten close to him on the racetrack, either. Linda's Chief, a dark bay colt by Chieftain, was the first foal of Dream Path, a daughter of Ambehaving that Hellman purchased privately from her owner and breeder, Joseph W. LaCroix. Though she debuted for Hellman with a $7,500 claiming tag, she finished second in the 1967 Spinaway Stakes and concluded her career with four wins from 13 starts and earnings of $42,175.

Trained by Al Scotti and ridden by Hall of Fame jockey Braulio Baeza, Linda's Chief won his debut by five lengths, then an allowance race by eight, tying the Belmont Park track record for 5 1/2 furlongs of 1:03 4/5 set just two weeks earlier by another two-year-old, Stop the Music.

When Linda's Chief won the $25,000-added Youthful Stakes by 2 1/2 lengths over Sailor Go Home and Stop the Music, June 12th, racing fans placed Hellman's colt at the head of his class in the East.

Linda's Chief confirmed their thinking by adding the $25,000-added Juvenile Stakes to his resume, rallying from third to score by half a length over Dust the Plate in a stakes record of 1:03 4/5 at Aqueduct.

Then Linda's Chief upped his record to five-for-five as the 2-5 favorite and 120-pound high weight in the $25,000-added Tremont Stakes at Aqueduct July 19th, defeating Dust the Plate by three-quarters of a length. Dust the Plate broke a front leg just past the finish line and had to be put down, a heartbreaking omen of Linda's Chief's fate.

Linda's Chief had already earned $59,850 while becoming the first undefeated two-year-old to sweep those three Juvenile stakes in New York. Lucky Draw swept those stakes in 1943, but he had previously suffered a defeat.

Linda's Chief had not. "He was a real nice horse, though he had a habit of drifting out a bit in the stretch," Baeza, now the assistant clerk of scales for the New York Racing Association, said in January 2004. "He had a lot of speed. That was his forte."

There is no more dizzying feeling in the world for a horse owner than having an unbeaten two-year-old. Nobody knows how good he is or will become. Hellman and Scotti penciled in the Sanford Stakes at Hellman's home track, Saratoga, for his next start.

Those who knew Hellman penciled in horse racing as just another successful business venture in a lifetime full of them.

Born on June 11, 1908, in an apartment opposite Albany

City Hall over Bender's Book Store, Hellman was the son of Harry and Nettie Hellman. The same year Neil Hellman was born, his parents, who owned a lighting appliance store, opened a nickelodeon, the first movie theater in Albany, and named it Fairyland. Fairyland eventually became the Royal Theater on South Pearl Street.

"I spent so much time at the Royal during the 1930s and the 1940s that when I close my eyes, I still can see the entire layout of the theater," Ruth Cohen, a life-long Albanian, wrote in a nostalgia piece in the Albany *Times Union*, November 25, 1984. She remembered Neil as usher, doorman, announcer and master of ceremonies for special attractions, like Dish Night and Ladies Gift Night. Such promotions were frequent in a highly competitive theater market.

Hellman once told *Times Union* reporter Carol DeMare that he "took tickets, was cashier, and ran bingo and bathing beauty contests . . . the whole ball of wax."

In a biographical sketch of Hellman in 1991, Virginia B. Bowers noted, "Thus his business career began with on-the-job training supervised by loving parents as teachers."

He began at an early age.

"His mother said he started working when he was nine," Neil Hellman's 93-year-old widow and wife of 54 years, Edith Marx Hellman, said in November 2003, at her daughter, Joyce, and son-in-law Sanford Bookstein's house in Albany.

On his way to becoming a remarkably successful businessman in many diverse fields and an incredibly generous philanthropist, Hellman's formal education ended with Albany High School. His real-life experience and unending work ethic more than made up for college. "My greatest pleasure in life is to work," he once said. "It's my biggest hobby."

He expected to succeed and he did. During the Depression in the 1930s, Hellman opened a chain of 10 women's apparel shops in Albany. According to Sanford Bookstein, Hellman purchased real estate in the 1930s and 1940s in Albany and Philadelphia "located in areas quite far from any centers of population to take advantage of low land cost. Subsequently, cities grew out to them, making the land valuable for commercial use."

Hellman had his own ideas about how to use that land. Movie theaters would be built in Albany, Philadelphia and Trenton, New Jersey.

In May 1941, Hellman opened his first drive-in theater in Latham, a city five miles north of Albany. He built another in Colonie, just west of Albany, in 1946, and two in Philadelphia in 1947 and 1949.

But entrepreneurial excitement did not last long for Hellman after he achieved success. So, many times in his life, he found new mountains to climb, even when he was the only person with the vision to see them. First it was dress shops. Then theaters. Then drive-in theaters. Then motels.

Sensing that urban sprawl would push people to find alternatives to staying in expensive, major downtown hotels, Hellman decided to build motels. "Everybody thought he was crazy," Edith Hellman said.

In May 1953, he opened the Mount Vernon Motel in East Greenbush, east of Albany. Two years later, he christened the Town House Motor Inn on Northern Boulevard in Albany's northern end. In 1957, he opened the million dollar Thruway Motor Inn on Washington Avenue, three miles from downtown Albany and across the street from the future home of the State University of New York at Albany's vast campus. The Thruway Motor Inn was reported in the *Times Union* to be "the first motel in the United States with color televisions in every room."

Then Hellman built a deluxe, 1,000-seat movie theater right next door and named it the Hellman Theater in memory of his father in 1960.

And then Hellman turned his attention to horse racing in the early 1960s. "Before he got involved in it, he enjoyed going to the track," Edith Hellman said. "He got friendly to the man sitting next to us, a judge. Then Neil decided he wanted to get involved. This gentleman suggested Dan Perlsweig as a trainer. Neil bought one horse and started claiming horses. It was fun. It was a challenge to him."

Betting was not. Hellman rarely bet on his own horses, and usually confined his wagering to $5 or $10 bets, telling reporters many times that the biggest bet he ever made was $50.

"I always enjoyed going to the races and seeing the horses run, though I was never much of a bettor," Hellman told Virginia Spain Spring in a story in the Schenectady *Union Star,* July 27, 1968. "But I got caught up on the challenge of the sport and decided to start my own stable."

He also bought his own farm in Ocala, Florida.

Hellman used a variety of trainers, including Perlsweig, Scotti, Johnny Campo, Tom Gullo and Buddy Jacobson. And Hellman took a hands-on approach, keeping condition books for racetracks where his horses were stabled. "He wanted to be involved in the day-to-day decisions, which was his nature, his personality, to be involved in his investments," his daughter, Joyce Hellman Bookstein, said. "To break into the establishment in those days was not always easy, but he worked at it." Hellman's other daughter, Barbara Hellman Iselin, also lives in Albany.

In the early to mid 1970s, when it was believed that the New York Racing Association was going to conduct an annual, earlier summer meet at Saratoga in addition to the August meet, Hellman pursued the possible rental of Saratoga Race Course. But instead of a second meet, NYRA stretched the four week August meet to the current six weeks from late July through Labor Day.

Hellman, though, quickly established a presence in Thoroughbred racing, first with Perlsweig and then with Jacobson, racing mostly claimers. The horse Hellman had the most fun with was Audience, a $10,000 claimer who won 18 races and was featured on the cover of the New York Racing Association track program. "My favorite is and always will be Audience," he told Albany *Times Union* columnist Tom Cunningham in 1981. But even with Audience, Hellman struggled to make a profit.

"They called Audience "The King of the Claimers," but Neil said he even lost money that year because of his other horses," Hellman's friend, Howard Nolan said in 2003. "He told me that story several times."

Nolan, a long time owner and breeder, was the State Senator from Albany County for 20 years, from 1975-1994 and is also a past president of the New York Thoroughbred Breeders, Inc. Nolan was a part owner of Argcangues, the long-shot winner of the 1993 Breeders' Cup Classic whose $2 win payoff of $269.20 remains the highest in Breeders' Cup history. Nolan has fond memories of Hellman. "Neil Hellman was a terrific person in my judgment," Nolan said. "He was very intelligent and a real man of his word. A lot of people in Albany didn't like him because he drove a tough bargain, but if he gave his word on something, it didn't even have to be written down. With Neil, his word really was his bond."

When he gave his word, it was after thoughtful consideration. "He was one of the most intelligent people I've ever met in my life," Nolan said. "He had a tremendous memory and a great ability to analyze figures."

Hellman did not like the figures his horses were producing. He knew he had to make a change if he hoped to make a profit.

Lenny Goodman, the agent for Baeza then and for Steve Cauthen in his Triple Crown sweep on Affirmed in 1978, suggested to Hellman that he give a few horses to Scotti. "Lenny kept after Neil, and Neil finally gave me a shot," Scotti, now retired at the age of 77, said in November 2003. "We got lucky right off the bat. He was the leading owner at Hialeah and Tropical Park and I was the leading trainer at Hialeah in 1968. We won 18 races, and they were claiming horses. It was unbelievable."

But Hellman and Scotti split ways temporarily, and in 1971, Hellman's Good Behaving, trained by Johnny Campo, won the Swift and Gotham Stakes before adding the $112,200 Wood Memorial that April 18th. The come-from-behind three-year-old won the Wood by a length under Chuck Baltazar at 5-

2 before a crowd of 51,303. Hellman was presented the winning trophy by U.S. Senator Jacob Javitz from New York.

Good Behaving skipped the Kentucky Derby, then ran 11th in a field of 13 to Pass Catcher in the Belmont Stakes under Ron Turcotte. Good Behaving's stable-mate, Jim French, finished second, and Cannonero II, seeking to become the first Triple Crown winner since Citation in 1948, was fourth as the 7-10 favorite.

Hellman also raced Good Behaving's stakes winning full brother, Mr. Paul B., and other stakes winners Wagon Dance, Gleaming Light and Laughing Bill, a horse he owned in partnership with Theodore Rosen.

Linda's Chief debuted in 1972 with Scotti as the trainer. "Neil called me and asked if I could take a couple horses for him," Scotti said. "That was the winter of 1971-1972. I took Linda's Chief as a two-year-old. He'd never run."

Scotti saw a difference in Hellman. "When I went back to work for him the second time, he was a different person," Scotti said. "We went away on trips together. Before, he was tough. You had to convince him you were right any time you wanted to do something. But the second time, he'd laugh and say, 'I'll go along with you, but don't make too many mistakes.'"

One thing hadn't changed. Hellman wanted to win races at Saratoga. "He'd rather win five races at Saratoga than 20 at Belmont Park," Scotti said.

Heading into the 1972 Sanford Stakes, Linda's Chief could not have been more accomplished: five wins in five starts, three of them stakes. "He was a hell of a horse," Scotti said. "He had tremendous speed. He had the two things you need to win races: speed and heart."

He also had Hellman's granddaughter's name. "He started naming horses for his grandchildren, then he stopped," Edith Hellman said. "He worried that if they did bad, it would embarrass them."

Linda's Chief had done nothing to embarrass the grandkids and would go off the 3-5 favorite in the Sanford field of five, which had just four betting interests because Northstar Dancer and Trevose were coupled as an entry. Sailor Go Home was another opponent. And Secretariat.

The luckiest moment in Virginia breeder/owner Christopher Chenery and his daughter Penny's lives came when he lost a coin flip.

The most influential sire in the 1960s was the Ogden Phipps' family's Bold Ruler, the leading stallion in progeny earnings in North America for seven consecutive seasons, 1963-1969. To enhance his value and get access to top broodmares they did not own, the Phipps made an arrangement with some of the owners of mares wishing to breed to him. If the mare was approved, she would be bred twice to Bold Ruler, producing, optimistically, two foals in two years. A coin flip would determine whether Phipps or the owner of the mare had first choice of the two.

But with Christopher Chenery, a family friend, the Phipps had a slightly different agreement, splitting four foals after two Chenery mares were bred to Bold Ruler in consecutive years. A coin toss would give the winner the choice of the first two; with the loser receiving the choice of the other two. The coin flip would also be used if there were only three foals instead of four.

In 1968, Chenery sent two mares, Somethingroyal and Hasty Matelda, to Bold Ruler. Somethingroyal had a filly; Hasty Matelda foaled a colt. In 1969, Chenery sent Somethingroyal and Cicada. Somethingroyal foaled a colt. Cicada was barren. Regardless, a coin toss at Belmont Park in the fall of 1969 determined who would have first choice of the foals. Ogden Phipps won the coin toss, and selected the filly Somethingroyal had foaled in 1969. Subsequently named The Bride, she raced four times without finishing better than sixth as a two-year-old and was retired. Chenery's Meadow Stable got stuck with the colt Hasty Matelda foaled in 1969—named Rising River, he had soundness problems and was sold for $50,000—and the foal Somethingroyal was carrying.

At 12:10 a.m. on March 30, 1970, a large chestnut colt

with three white feet and a stripe on his forehead left the womb of Somethingroyal and greeted his new world. He was on his feet in 20 minutes and starting nursing 25 minutes later.

There's an old poem on the backstretch about horses with white feet:

> One white foot, run him for life;
> Two white feet, keep him for your wife;
> Three white feet, keep him for your man;
> Four white feet, sell him if you can;
> Four white feet and a stripe on the nose;
> Knock him on the head and feed him to the crows.

Somethingroyal's foal was a keeper, one who needed a name. The Jockey Club rejected the first five names submitted by Meadow Stable: Scepter, Royal Line, Something Special, Games of Chance, and Deo Volente (Latin for god willing). The final name, suggested by Chenery's corporate and personal secretary, Elizabeth Ham, was Secretariat.

Secretariat was shipped to Meadow Stable trainer Lucien Laurin's barn at Hialeah Park in Florida on January 10, 1972. His first groom, Mordechai "Pop" Williams, was succeeded by Eddie Sweat, who was also the groom of Meadow Stable's Kentucky Derby hopeful Riva Ridge.

Riva Ridge would go on to win the 1972 Derby and Belmont Stakes under Ron Turcotte, who, like Laurin, was from Canada. Destined to be a lumberjack with his dad after dropping out of high school in Grand Falls, New Brunswick, Turcotte changed his future by striking out to Toronto. Almost out of money, he took any job he could find. One of them was searching a golf course every night for worms he could sell to fishermen. That did not produce a lot of revenue, and he was a day away from returning home when someone asked him, "Have you ever thought of becoming a jockey?"

Turcotte became one of the best jockeys ever, landing in the Hall of Fame in a career cut short when he was paralyzed from the waist down in an accident in the eighth race at Belmont Park, July 13, 1978. Unwilling to let that stop his life,

Turcotte returned to Canada with his devoted wife, Gae, and raised three daughters. Turcotte even went back to high school in Van Buren, Maine, just across the border, to get his diploma, May 17, 1990, at the age of 48. His willingness to do so sparked headlines in newspapers around the country.

Every August, he drives his specially-designed van from New Brunswick, Canada, to Saratoga Springs to attend the annual Hall of Fame inductions at the National Museum of Racing and visit with old friends. Invariably, fans will ask him to sign photos or old pari-mutuel tickets they never cashed on Secretariat.

"I had high hopes for this horse all along, ever since I galloped him at Hialeah," Turcotte said in November 2003. "Lucien showed me the horses that had just come in. He told me to look at that red horse. He was the most loveable animal, like a big overgrown kid. He wouldn't shy away from anything. He just took everything in stride. The first time I worked him, he didn't remember which foot to put down first. But each time was better and better."

But Turcotte would miss Secretariat's first two starts.

When Secretariat made his debut at Aqueduct, July 4, 1972, Turcotte was at Monmouth Park, winning the Monmouth Oaks on Summer Guest for trainer Elliott Burch. Apprentice Paul Feliciano would ride Secretariat, who was sent off the tepid 3-1 favorite in a field of 12 from the rail. It was an eventful journey.

A horse named Quebec ducked in sharply from the three post at the start, slamming into the '2' horse, Strike the Line, who slammed into Secretariat, nearly sending him into the rail. Secretariat recovered almost immediately, but got stalled in traffic on the far turn. Feliciano finally found room on the inside, and then Secretariat got blocked in the final 70 yards. He finished fourth by a length and a quarter. The comment in the Daily Racing Form said he finished "full of run," a testimony to the 7 1/2 lengths Secretariat had made up rallying from 10th, while also noting that he had been impeded.

Two days later, Turcotte was in the hospital after a

horse he'd been riding at Aqueduct suffered a heart attack during a race, leaving Turcotte with contusions of his lungs, back and chest.

So Feliciano got another chance, and, on July 15th at Aqueduct, Secretariat won a maiden race by six lengths as the 6-5 favorite.

Turcotte rode Secretariat in his next start, an allowance race at Saratoga on Opening Day, July 31st. Sent off at 2-5, Secretariat won by a length and a half. "I let him drop back," Turcotte said. "When I called on him, he responded. He won very easy."

In the Sanford Stakes, Secretariat was the 1.50-to-1 second choice. Linda's Chief was 3-5. "I've got to believe, in my heart, Linda's Chief was the sentimental favorite," Scotti said. "Neil was a big man up there. And he's very big with the politicians. Everybody knew him. I've still got to believe, with the sharp bettors, if they ran at Belmont, Secretariat would have been favored. Everybody knew Secretariat was a tiger. Once he got rolling, he was like a truck. He was such a monster of a horse."

Tom Conoby, who works with Bob Gersowitz in Albany, had the good fortune of being at Aqueduct when Secretariat made his debut. "When he took the track, he looked like Arnold Schwarzenegger," Conoby said. "I knew I was looking at something out of the ordinary. I bet him. That's why I went back and saw his second race."

Conoby wound up attending 16 of Secretariat's 21 races.

Gersowitz and Conoby, who didn't know each other at the time, watched Secretariat get saddled for the Sanford. "He was chiseled," Gersowitz said. "Ray Charles could have seen how good he looked."

Secretariat didn't look that good at the quarter pole, with just two furlongs of the six-furlong Sanford remaining. Entry-mates Trevose, ridden by Eddie Belmonte, and Northstar Dancer, ridden by Angel Cordero, Jr., were shoulder to shoulder, first and second, with Secretariat waiting for room behind them. "Belmonte was on the rail and Cordero was alongside," Turcotte said. "I was sitting there with no place to go."

Then Trevose and Northstar Dancer began drifting apart. "Cordero wanted to keep the hole closed," Turcotte said. "Belmonte hollered at Cordero, 'Ronnie's coming through! Ronnie's coming through!' So Cordero swerved in and Belmonte came out. I was already going through. He went through them like a halfback. They just ricocheted off me. He won easy."

Secretariat won by three lengths, while Linda's Chief rallied under Baeza to finish second, six lengths ahead of Northstar Dancer in third. "We were disappointed, but I don't think we were surprised," Sanford Bookstein, said.

Baeza thought Linda's Chief was in a good position early in the race. "He was looking pretty good until Secretariat came alongside him," Baeza said. "Then he didn't look so good. I had a good look at Secretariat's rear end."

Mark Cusano, a handicapper and host of a weekly OTB cable television show "Down The Stretch," remembered reading a quote from Scotti the next day in a newspaper: "They asked him where Linda's Chief was going next, and he said, 'Anywhere that big red horse doesn't go.'"

Thirty-one years later, Scotti confirmed that was exactly what he did tell reporters. "I convinced Neil to duck Secretariat," Scotti said. "Neil had a lot of pride, so it was hard to convince him, but I did. We couldn't beat him."

But they did try Big Red one more time that fall. After winning an allowance race and finishing third behind Step Nicely and Stop the Music in the Cowdin Stakes at Belmont Park, Linda's Chief was one of 11 two-year-olds to challenge Secretariat in the $125,000 Champagne Stakes at Belmont, October 14th.

Secretariat had followed his victory in the Sanford with a sensational win in the Hopeful Stakes at Saratoga, sitting last in the field of nine, then circling the entire field on the turn while racing five to six-wide and drawing off to a five length victory. He followed with a 1 3/4 length win in the Futurity Stakes at Belmont and would go off the 3-5 favorite in the Champagne coupled with Angle Light, also trained by Laurin. Step Nicely was the 6-1 second choice and Linda's Chief the 8-1 third choice under Laffit Pincay, Jr.

Secretariat beat Stop the Music by two lengths, but was disqualified for lightly bumping him just inside the three-sixteenths pole in the stretch. Secretariat was placed second, making Stop the Music the winner, a controversial decision Turcotte still feels was unjust. Linda's Chief finished a soundly beaten fifth and Hellman decided to ship Linda's Chief to California for the 1972-1973 winter, where he raced in the care of Bobby Frankel. "Lenny Goodman talked me into using Bobby Frankel," Scotti said. "We were all from Brooklyn, all three of us. He did a hell of a job with Linda's Chief."

Linda's Chief won the 1973 San Miguel Stakes in a Santa Anita track record of 1:33 4/5 for the mile, January 18th, then finished second in the San Vincente to Ancient Title. Linda's Chief then won three straight, a minor stakes, the San Jacinto Stakes at 4-5 and the San Felipe Stakes at even money. Ancient Title was second in the last two.

Having won 10 of 14 starts, Linda's Chief went off the 3-5 favorite in the 1973 Santa Anita Derby, finishing second to Sham.

Sham, in turn, finished second to Secretariat in the Kentucky Derby and Preakness Stakes before finishing last to him in the Belmont Stakes, when Secretariat completed the first Triple Crown in 25 years with an astounding 31-length win which cemented his equine immortality.

Linda's Chief won the California Derby at Golden Gate Fields, April 21, then returned to New York, winning the 1973 Withers Stakes under Jorge Velazquez at one mile over Stop the Music and Forego. "He stumbled leaving the gate and he still won in 1:34 and four (4/5)," Scotti said, a trace of pride still evident in his voice three decades later. That's because Forego went on to be named Horse of the Year in 1974, 1975 and 1976.

Linda's Chief was the last Thoroughbred who beat the great gelding at equal weights.

Avoiding Secretariat, Scotti shipped Linda's Chief to Chicago, and he won the Pontiac Grand Prix in mid-June. Linda's Chief followed that with a win in the Saranac Stakes at Aqueduct.

His career record then was 12 wins, three seconds and a third in 17 starts, and Hellman, ever the businessman, sold his prize colt for $1.8 million to Aaron Jones, a prominent owner who made his mark in lumber, establishing the Seneca Timber Country and Seneca Sawmill Company, one of the world's largest, in the Pacific Northwest. At the time, Jones's purchase was the highest ever paid for a horse still racing.

Jones and his wife, Marie, would later campaign champions Lehigh Gold, Tiffany Lass and Riboletta, but Linda's Chief won just one of 11 starts for them, and that was in his first start for his new owners, a bet-less, three-horse $15,000 exhibition allowance race at Monmouth Park, July 26th, ostensibly a prep race for the $100,000 Monmouth Invitational Handicap nine days later. The prep did not help. Linda's Chief finished fifth to Our Native as the 3-5 favorite in the Monmouth Invitational.

After Linda's Chief finished third behind Step Nicely and Forego in the one mile Jerome Handicap, spotting the two horses eight and two pounds, respectively, Jones shipped Linda's Chief back to California and placed him in the care of Hall of Fame trainer Charlie Whittingham.

Linda's Chief went winless in his first seven starts as a four-year-old, bearing out badly in the last one, before he was entered in the Los Angeles Handicap, May 11, 1974. While battling for the lead early in the seven furlong race, Linda's Chief propped, throwing jockey Steve Valdez. Linda's Chief "took a few more strides, then attempted to jump the rail and toppled over," Leon Rasmussen wrote in the *Thoroughbred Record* (now the *Thoroughbred Times*), May 18, 1974. "He fell in a heap before 37,000 shocked, chilled and hushed fans, and remained motionless throughout the race. Veterinarians John Peters and

Jock Jocoy reached the stricken animal almost immediately and were quickly joined by Dr. Alan Edmondson. All agreed the son of Chieftain had broken his back and was paralyzed. Of course, it was necessary to euthanize him. He was said to have been insured for $2 million. . . . Fortunately, Valdez suffered nothing more than bruised knees."

Yet Linda Chief's life continues to have an impact on people today, three decades later. For Hellman took the money from selling his Thoroughbred and, in 1975, donated $2,075,000 to Albany Medical College and the Albany Medical Center Hospital, the largest gift ever received by the two affiliated institutions.

The gift had no restrictions, and $500,000 of the donation was used in the hospital to set up the first computer-linked brain scan laboratory in upstate New York. Another portion of the gift was used to create the $1 million Neil Hellman Cardiac Catheterization Laboratory at Albany Medical Center Hospital.

Hellman would have never spent that kind of money on himself. "Neil was not ostentatious in any way," Howard Nolan said. "He had a modest house, and he drove a nice car, but nothing ostentatious by any means. He was a simple guy in the sense that he didn't enjoy the glitter. That was him."

So was giving back.

Though Jewish, Hellman, in 1982, donated $500,000 for the Neil Hellman Library to the College of Saint Rose, the largest single gift a Catholic college had ever received. And though Hellman wasn't African-American, he created a scholarship fund exclusively for African-American students in memory of Mae Douglas, a black woman who worked at his home.

In 1984, Hellman donated $300,000 for a new educational facility at Parsons Child and Family Center in Albany for children with special needs and their families. It would be called the Neil Hellman School. "He wanted to give back to the community," Sanford Bookstein said. "It was as simple as that."

Giving money away wasn't as simple as one might

think. "He said it was easier to make money than give it away," Hellman's daughter, Joyce Bookstein, said.

Yet he did.

Hellman spent 42 years of his adult life supporting Camp Thatcher, and was also active in the Albany Boys Club, the March of Dimes, the American Cancer Society, the United Jewish Appeal and the Arthritis Foundation.

"He did say, 'Well, I don't have sons, and I want the Hellman name to be prominent,'" Edith Hellman said of her husband of 54 years. "His father died of cancer. I think that was on his mind. And he always loved children."

In an interview with Carol DeMare of the Albany *Times Union*, Hellman explained his philanthropy: "The people in the Capital District who have made it possible for me to amass the amount of money I have . . . I want to do something to repay them, and there is no greater way of doing it than to provide in some way the best of care."

In 1984, Neil Hellman received an honorary degree of Doctor of Science from the Albany Medical College.

He died of cardiac arrest at the Albany Medical Center Hospital, April 24, 1985.

"He was a fun loving, charismatic human being," his daughter, Joyce said. "He was just as happy talking to a plumber as the head of Albany Med. He was also a very family conscious man, and he respected females. We have a daughter who is an attorney. So many men of that generation did not have the same respect for professional females."

Linda's Chief, whom Hellman once said had "never run a dishonest race in his life," was not Hellman's last top horse. In 1974, Hellman's Laughing Bridge won the Schuylerville Stakes on opening day and the Adirondack Stakes at Saratoga before finishing second by 12 3/4 lengths to the brilliant, undefeated Ruffian in the Spinaway Stakes, yet another superstar a Hellman horse encountered.

Hellman's interest in racing waned through the 1970s, and, in 1980, he sold most of his horses as well as his farm in

Ocala, Florida. "He enjoyed it, but he finally got tired of it," Sanford Bookstein said.

Hellman had raced the only horse ever favored over Secretariat and rued that they were the same age. "Neil wasn't the only one," his wife Edith said. "It was a bad year for anyone with a three-year-old."

Affirmed (inside) holds off Alydar to win the
1978 Belmont Stakes and the Triple Crown.
(*Photo Courtesy of Adam Coglianese*)

CHAPTER 3

Last Dance

'Wish I didn't know now
What I didn't know then.'
—Bob Seger, "Against The Wind"

When you go to the racetrack, you know you might leave feeling ecstatic, disconsolate or in a mood somewhere in between. You never expect to walk out feeling empty.

That's what happened on a late August afternoon at Saratoga Race Course in 1978, when the greatest rivalry in modern Thoroughbred racing became the greatest disappointment; when one of the world's greatest riders, Laffit Pincay, Jr., made the poorest judgment decision of his extraordinary career.

By the time they shipped to Saratoga as two-year-old colts in the summer of 1977, Patrice and Louis Wolfson's Harbor View Farm's Affirmed, trained by Laz Barrera and ridden by 17-year-old apprentice sensation Steve Cauthen, and Calumet Farm's Alydar, ridden by Jorge Velazquez for trainer John Veitch, had already tested each other twice, splitting decisions.

Affirmed, a handsome chestnut by Exclusive Native, out of Won't Tell You, by Crafty Admiral, had an experience edge over Alydar when they first met in the Youthful Stakes at

Belmont Park, June 15, 1977. Affirmed had already won his May 24th debut, wire-to-wire from the 10 post under Bernie Gonzalez by 4 1/2 lengths at odds of 14-1. The Youthful was his second career start, yet he would not be favored in the 5 1/2 furlong Youthful Stakes under Angel Cordero, Jr., going off at 3.40-to-1 in the field of 11.

The favorite, despite making his debut in stakes company, was the striking colt Alydar, a dark chestnut son of Raise a Native (who was also Affirmed's paternal grand-sire), out of Sweet Tooth, by On-and-On. Under Eddie Maple, who rode Alydar in his first seven starts, Alydar went off at 9-5. He closed six lengths in the stretch, but that was only good enough for fifth, five lengths behind Affirmed, who had narrowly defeated Wood Native by a neck.

Veitch gave Alydar a start in a maiden race nine days later at Belmont, and he won by 6 3/4 lengths.

When Alydar and Affirmed met again in the Great American, another 5 1/2 furlong stakes at Belmont, July 6th, Alydar was again made the favorite, an odds-on favorite at 4-5. Affirmed went off at 9-2 in the field of seven, led early and was dueled into defeat by Alydar, who beat his rival by 3 1/2 lengths.

That made them 1-1 in their rivalry, and already fans were heavily debating which of the two-year-olds was better. Everybody knew they were outstanding colts already, and each strengthened that sentiment by going undefeated until their third meeting in the Hopeful Stakes at Saratoga, August 27th.

Barrera, who raced his stable in California and New York, shipped Affirmed to Hollywood Park for his next start. With Pincay up, Affirmed took the six furlong Juvenile Championship by seven lengths as the 2-5 favorite. Returned to New York, Affirmed won the Sanford Stakes at Saratoga by 2 3/4 lengths under Cauthen. Affirmed had won the Juvenile Championship wire-to-wire, but rallied from three lengths back at the half to win the Sanford going away in a quick 1:09 3/5 for six furlongs. He was speedy, versatile and had four wins and a second in his first five starts.

Alydar also raced twice more before the Hopeful. After winning the Tremont Stakes by a length and a quarter, getting six furlongs in 1:10, Alydar shipped south to New Jersey to contest the Grade 1 Sapling Stakes at Monmouth Parks over a sloppy track. Veitch added blinkers for Alydar's fifth career start, and went along for the ride, even though he also sent out Calumet Farm's outstanding three-year-old filly Our Mims in the Grade 1 Alabama Stakes at Saratoga the same afternoon. Veitch entrusted Our Mims to his dad, Hall of Fame trainer Sylvester Veitch. "Alydar was a two-year-old and he was ship-ping for the first time," John Veitch explained. "I thought Our Mims had a great chance of winning the Alabama, but Alydar looked like he was going to be a very useful horse at the time. Since he was making his first road trip, I thought it was more important for me to be there for him. I wanted to do every-thing right for him. When you send a nice horse on the road for the first time, you don't know how he's going to take the trip. Even those days in his two-year-old year, we had great hopes for him. Mrs. Markey (co-owner of Calumet Farm with her husband, Admiral Gene Markey), particularly with her age—she was in her 80s—wanted to have another great horse. She was concerned about him. She was from the old school: doing what was right for the horse. She took a very active interest in her horses. She liked to talk about them and she liked to be kept abreast about them."

On August 13, 1977, she and the Admiral enjoyed a rare double, winning Grade 1 stakes at two different tracks almost simultaneously. Our Mims won the Alabama by a neck, while Alydar had no trouble in his first race on a wet track, winning the Sapling by 2 1/2 lengths. That gave him a four race win-ning streak heading into the Hopeful, the lone blemish in his career the fifth in a stakes debut behind Affirmed. That would be the only time in their 10 meetings that they did not finish 1-2 or 2-1.

In their third meeting in the 73rd running of the $80,175 Hopeful Stakes, on closing day at Saratoga, August 27th,

Alydar would be favored for the third time, going off at even money in the field of five going six and a half furlongs. The Hopeful drew its name from being the first stakes race farther than six furlongs for two-year-olds. Hopeful winners frequently made an impact in the Triple Crown the following year, such as 1972 winner Secretariat, on the way to the 1973 Triple Crown, and 1974 winner Foolish Pleasure, who won the 1975 Kentucky Derby.

Affirmed went off at 2.30-to-1. Darby Creek Road 4-1, speedy Tilt Up 5-1 and Regal And Royal 9-1.

Affirmed broke first, but quickly surrendered the lead to Tilt Up, ridden by Jacinto Vasquez. Angel Cordero, Jr., sent Darby Creek Road into second while Cauthen settled Affirmed in third and Maple had Alydar, who was steadied early, in fourth.

Tilt Up went the first quarter in :22 4/5, then had to run the second quarter even faster, :22 2/5, to maintain a head lead over Darby Creek Road and Affirmed through a half in :45 1/5. Maple took Alydar to the far outside and he quickly closed in.

Darby Creek Road failed to sustain his bid, and Affirmed caught Tilt Up before mid-stretch, when he was immediately confronted by Alydar. Alydar got within a head of Affirmed, but no closer as Affirmed grittily held on to a precarious lead. Just before the wire, Affirmed was inching away from Alydar, crossing the wire a half length in front after setting a stakes record of 1:15 2/5, faster than the winning times of Secretariat (1:16 1/5) and Foolish Pleasure (1:16). Affirmed stakes' record still stands. It was threatened only by Great Navigator (1:15 3/5) and Dehere (1:15 4/5) in 1992 and 1993, before the distance of the Hopeful was extended to seven furlongs in 1994.

"In the stretch, when he looked Tilt Up in the eye, he just went on," Cauthen said. "He had a good finishing kick."

So did Barrera. Destined for the Hall of Fame, Barrera won that afternoon's fourth race and the Hopeful to tie with Tommy Kelly for the trainer's title with eight victories. Barrera had won the title the previous two years.

Affirmed and Alydar faced each other again in the seven furlong Futurity at Belmont Park. For the first time, Affirmed was a slight favorite at 6-5 (1.20-to-1) with Alydar 3-2 (1.50-to-1). Again, they staged a heavyweight, head-to-head battle for the final four furlongs, Affirmed led by a head, then Alydar pushed a head in front. But Affirmed came on again and beat Alydar by a nose.

Alydar enacted revenge in the one mile Champagne Stakes at Belmont exactly one month later as they went off the exact same odds as in the Futurity. Ridden for the first time by Velasquez, Alydar rolled up on the outside of Affirmed on the far turn and swept past, winning by a length and a quarter. The series was now 3-2, Affirmed.

One final meeting would determine the two-year-old championship, the mile and a sixteenth Laurel Futurity in Maryland, October 29th. This time, Alydar was pounded down to odds of 2-5 (.40-to-1) with Affirmed 7-5 (1.40-to-1). Affirmed won by a neck, marking the fourth time in their six meetings that the favored of the two lost. There was a 10 length gap to Star de Naskra in third, reflecting the difference in ability of both Affirmed and Alydar and the other two-year-olds in America. Affirmed, who led the series, 4-2, was rightfully voted Two-Year-Old Champion and headed to California to prepare for his three-year-old season. Veitch gave Alydar one more start, a second by two lengths to Believe It in the Remsen Stakes at Aqueduct on a sloppy track, before shipping him to Florida to prepare for his three-year-old battles with Affirmed. They would not meet again until the Kentucky Derby, leaving their fans months to argue over who would be the better three-year-old.

Veitch plotted his strategy to get there with the Markeys. "I knew they wanted to run in the Flamingo Stakes, which was run first those days, and the Florida Derby, then the Blue Grass, which is kind of traditional with Calumet being down the road from Keeneland," Veitch said. It would give them an opportunity, and, as it worked out, their only opportunity, to see Alydar run live."

Veitch couldn't have been happier as Alydar's three-year-old season unfolded. "I thought he was becoming stronger all through his three-year-old season," he said. "In his winter in Florida, everything went perfect for him. He was impressive and he became more professional. He did every thing you would want a colt to do early in his three-year-old season."

Both horses had four races leading up to the Kentucky Derby.

Alydar won an allowance race by two lengths, the Flamingo by 4 1/2, the Florida Derby by two lengths and, at odds of 1-10, the Blue Grass Stakes by 13 lengths after he visited with Mrs. Markey. "They let Mrs. Markey take her car up to the very edge of the track to see the race," Veitch said. "I told Jorge Velasquez to take the horse as close to the rail as he could coming out of the post parade. And he did. It had been cleared with the stewards. Jorge took Alydar up there and said, 'Here's your horse, my lady.' Then the horse looked like he dropped his head a little bit. It was very poignant."

Affirmed's winter was very wet. Rain forced Barrera to repeatedly juggle Affirmed's plans. But he kept winning, taking an allowance race by five lengths, the San Felipe Stakes by two, the Santa Anita Derby by eight lengths and the Hollywood Derby by two lengths, all four at odds of 1-5.

The Kentucky Derby was next.

Alydar brought in a record of 10 wins and four seconds in his last 14 starts after finishing fifth behind Affirmed in his debut.

Affirmed had 11 wins and two seconds in 13 starts.

Fans argued over who would be favored. Alydar was at 6-5 (1.20-to-1). Affirmed was 9-5 (1.80-to-1). Affirmed settled in third in the field of 11, while Alydar fell 17 lengths back in ninth. Affirmed moved first to take the lead and Alydar continued a sustained rally. Affirmed held him off by a length and a half.

The Preakness was much tighter. Affirmed, favored at 1-2 (.50-to-1), set the pace, and Alydar, sent off at 9-5

(1.80-to-1), roared up from sixth to second on the turn as if he would engulf Affirmed. But Affirmed had plenty left and held off Alydar by a neck.

Their race in the Belmont Stakes was one for the ages, one of the greatest races of all time with Affirmed seeking the Triple Crown. Veitch decided to remove Alydar's blinkers. "It was a mile and a half race," Veitch said. "I wanted him to relax a little bit more, to be more manageable. I looked back in history. So many horses in the Belmont, if they got an easy lead and were genuine, you were at a real disadvantage. And Affirmed certainly was genuine. I told Jorge that coming out of the first turn, I wanted to be right on him. Take the battle to him. That was the plan."

Alydar went off the 1.10-to-1 second choice in the field of five. Affirmed was 3-5 (.60-to-1).

Velasquez followed Veitch's directions, staying on Affirmed's flank the entire backstretch run before going after him on the turn. And then they did it again: shoulder-to-shoulder, eye-to-eye the entire length of the Belmont stretch. "I thought I had him beat at the eighth pole," Veitch said.

He did. Alydar stuck a nose in front before Affirmed did what he always did: find more. One hundred yards from the finish line, they were dead even. By the wire, Affirmed had a desperate head in front, completing the Triple Crown. "They could have run all the way to China and Alydar wasn't going to get past him," a joyous Barrera said afterwards.

Alydar had made history by running second in all three Triple Crown races and pushing Affirmed to his absolute limit. Affirmed had taken a 7-2 lead in the series. They would meet again in the Travers at Saratoga, and neither Veitch nor Alydar's fans were ready to concede to Affirmed. Not yet. Thoroughbreds continue to grow and develop through their three-year-old season, and, Alydar rebounded from the Belmont Stakes so incredibly well that his backers took new hope.

Maybe the Travers would be different.

Few three-year-olds can withstand competing in all

three Triple Crown races, and the ones that do are usually spent after the Belmont Stakes. Not Alydar.

"I had planned not to run Alydar before Saratoga, but I backed off his training and he wouldn't have it," Veitch said. "He was so much better when he came out of the Belmont than when he went into the Derby. Other horses show me wear and tear. He was saying, 'Give me more, boss.' I told the Markeys, 'I don't want to squeeze the lemon, but we have to do something with him.'"

Veitch picked the Arlington Classic at Arlington Park, July 22nd. Four equine sacrifices were gathered and Alydar blew them away, winning the mile and a quarter stakes by 13 lengths with Jeff Fell subbing for Velasquez.

That set up Alydar for Saratoga, and Veitch chose the Whitney Handicap against older horses on August 5th, rather than the traditional prep for the Travers, the Jim Dandy Stakes against three-year-olds, three days later. "The timing for Alydar was better in the Whitney, even though there were older horses," Veitch said.

One of them, the four-year-old J. O. Tobin, had delivered Seattle Slew's first career loss the summer before when he won the Swaps Stakes at Hollywood Park by eight lengths and Seattle Slew, making his first start since becoming the only undefeated winner of the Triple Crown, finished fourth by 16 lengths.

In 1978, J. O. Tobin had won five of six starts, the only miss a fourth to Exceller in the Hollywood Gold Cup. In his last start before the Whitney, he won the seven furlong Tom Fool Handicap by 6 1/2 lengths at 6-5. Yet he would go off at 5-2 in the Whitney at the mile and an eighth. Alydar was 3-5 and ran that well, making an explosive sweep of the field inside horses on the turn and winning by 10 lengths in 1:47 2/5, only two-fifths of a second off Tri Jet's still standing 1974 track record.

"I was more confident going into the Travers than I was in any race with Alydar," Veitch said. "Coming into the Travers, although I'd gotten beat in the Triple Crown, I felt I'm invincible. Then I looked at Affirmed in the Jim Dandy."

Three days after the Whitney, Affirmed went off the 1-20 favorite (.05-to-1) in a field of five and looked absolutely beaten. It was his first start since the Belmont Stakes, and he was sluggish, falling eight lengths off a horse loose on the lead, Sensitive Prince. Trained by Hall of Famer Allen "Giant Killer" Jerkens, whose horses upset Secretariat twice and Kelso three times, Sensitive Prince had finished a distant sixth to Affirmed in the Kentucky Derby at equal weights. In the Jim Dandy, he carried nine pounds less and seemed home free at the top of the stretch with a four length lead. With just an eighth of a mile left, Sensitive Prince was still three lengths ahead. At the six-teenth pole, Sensitive Prince still led by two lengths. It looked hopeless for Affirmed, yet he surged powerfully to win by half a length in a stakes record 1:47 4/5. "I thought it was one of his greatest races," Patrice Wolfson said in January, 2004.

Veitch was rooting for Affirmed the whole way. "I wanted him to win," Veitch said. "I was rooting for him because I wanted him to come into the Travers unblemished. If anybody was going to draw first blood on him, I wanted it to be Alydar. I'd been watching Affirmed for a year and a half. I thought the Triple Crown took something out of him. It could have been wishful thinking on my part, but I was more confi-dent than ever in the Travers."

The stage had been set for Saratoga's Mid-Summer Derby. Only Pincay, not Cauthen, would be riding Affirmed the afternoon of August 19, 1978. Cauthen injured his shoul-der and knee in a spill on a horse named Cute As A Button at Saratoga August 9th, and would watch the 109th running of the Travers in a suit standing next to Patrice Wolfson. Only two other three-year-olds entered the Travers, Nasty and Bold and Shake Shake Shake.

This was all about Alydar-Affirmed. Equal Weights. Mile and a Quarter. Round Ten. Affirmed led, 7-2.

Affirmed's career record heading into the Travers was 15 wins, including nine straight, and two seconds to Alydar in 17 starts. Alydar had 11 wins and seven seconds, six of them to Affirmed, in 18 starts following the fifth to Affirmed in his career debut.

It does not get any better than that.

Affirmed, who worked a mile in 1:40 2/5 four days before the Travers, would go off the favorite at 3-5 (.70-to-1). Alydar, who worked six furlongs in 1:13 and then a half in :47 3/5 the day before the race, was even money (1.00-to-1). A then-record crowd of 50,359, more than 15,000 over the record set for the 1977 Travers, when Run Dusty Run nosed Jatski but was disqualified and placed second, packed Saratoga Race Course. Wisely, the New York Racing Association opened the infield to handle the overflow of fans.

Just about every one of them gasped in mid-race. Affirmed had passed Shake Shake Shake, ridden by Cordero, on the backstretch to take the lead. Shake Shake Shake then began to drift out as he tired. Seeing this, Velasquez moved Alydar up the inside.

Just past the half-mile pole, Alydar moved within a neck of Affirmed. Then, suddenly, the horses brushed as Pincay and Affirmed closed the rail, cutting off Alydar severely. Velasquez, in a display of deft horsemanship, gathered up Alydar, snatching him back to the outside to avoid running right into Affirmed.

"It scared me to death," Veitch said. "I thought he'd broken down. Alydar's head went up and I thought he broke a leg. Then Jorge got him to run again."

Though he had nearly come to a complete stop, Alydar took off after Affirmed, who had opened a substantial lead of maybe five lengths when Alydar was forced to check. Alydar closed the gap to a length and three-quarters at the finish line, a great display of courage.

Of course, the Inquiry light went on immediately on the tote board. Then the sign saying "Objection."

Anyone and everyone knew what would happen next. The stewards' decision was a no-brainer. There was no controversy, because Affirmed's foul had been blatant. He was disqualified and placed second and Alydar move up to first.

"I did not want to win it that way," Velasquez told reporters. "Please excuse me. I'm very upset right now."

Pincay called the stewards' decision "borderline. I saw Velasquez coming up on the inside of me. However, I did not think there was enough room for him to get through."

There sure wasn't after Pincay cut him off, a rare lapse in judgment by a brilliant rider. "The thing that really upsets me is that there's enough chance of injury without this," Veitch said after the race. "Jorge said he was within an inch of being dropped. Alydar's head brushed the rump of Affirmed. They might be able to do that in California, but not here."

Even Barrera the next day acknowledged to the Associated Press that the disqualification was valid: "His number had to come down." Years later, Pincay would say, "I didn't realize he was that close. It was one of the lowest points in my career."

A quarter of a century has not extinguished Veitch's disappointment. "That's not the way it was supposed to be," he said in 2003. "I wanted Alydar to vindicate himself. It was just kind of taken away. There isn't a race that has left a more bitter taste in myself. I'm still bitter. Revenge is not the right word, but Alydar should have had his satisfaction."

Asked if he had any satisfaction from being placed first, Veitch quietly said, "No."

In January 2004, Patrice Wolfson said of the 1978 Travers, "It had no significance, except to cause chaos."

Arguments about who would have won the race without the incident are utterly pointless.

Nobody knows. And nobody ever will. We were cheated from finding out and then sent home. The only thing that made it the slightest bit bearable was not knowing that Affirmed and Alydar would never race against each other again.

Move It Now, Ruben Hernandez up.
(*Photo Courtesy of Bonnie von Wiesenthal*)

CHAPTER 4

Left Behind

As he walked Move It Now behind the starting gate, waiting to be the last horse to load in the outside 11 stall in the $100,000 DeWitt Clinton Stakes at Saratoga Race Course, August 6, 1980, jockey Ruben Hernandez was focused on the task ahead. One of New York's top jockeys, he knew he would have to use Move It Now's abundant early speed to get position before the first turn in the mile and an eighth race. Failing to do so would mean getting caught wide on the turn and losing precious ground she might not be able to make up.

Though he was riding a filly against colts, Hernandez was confident. She had already beaten males earlier in the year, taking the Albany Handicap, another stakes for three-year-old New York-breds, at Aqueduct by a nose over another filly, Screenland, the favorite in the DeWitt Clinton. The Albany Handicap had a $50,000 purse. The DeWitt Clinton's purse was double that, the first $100,000 race ever for New York-breds.

Bettors believed Move It Now, who had a record of four wins, three seconds and a fourth in eight career starts, was the horse to beat, making her the 5-2 second choice in the field of 11.

Because the race was the same distance as the circumference of Saratoga's main track, fans would get a good view of the start of the DeWitt Clinton.

A lot better than Hernandez's.

"I was the last one to load," he said. "And they kept loading and loading. There were three horses left, then two. I was about 10 feet from the gate. They kept saying, 'One more, one more.' It's time to walk into the gate. And all of a sudden, 'RRRRRRINNNNNG!'"

Hernandez, still on Move It Now behind the starting gate, looked up in disbelief. The DeWitt Clinton had started without him. "It was like a dream," Hernandez said. "I couldn't believe it."

Neither could her breeder, John Hettinger, who was at Saratoga that afternoon. "I said, 'Let's get out of here,'" he said 23 years later. "It was disappointing."

Hettinger, chairman of the Grayson-Jockey Club Research Foundation and a member of the Board of the Fasig-Tipton Sales Company, has been at the forefront of the Thoroughbred racing industry's recent, on-going battle to end the slaughter of horses for human consumption in the United States. Also a member of The Jockey Club and the New York Racing Association Board of Trustees, Hettinger has been a prominent breeder at his Akindale Farm, in Pawling, New York, since the inception of the New York State Thoroughbred Breeding and Development Fund in 1973. He has nothing but fond memories of Move It Now, a daughter of Timeless Moment, out of Warfingers by Warfare, who was foaled at Akindale. "She was the first really good horse we bred," he said in October 2003. "Jim Maloney trained her. He was one of my great heroes."

Maloney, inducted into the National Museum of Racing Hall of Fame in 1963, trained 42 stakes winners in a career spanning 50 years, from 1935 until his death in 1984. The son of a trainer, Maloney opened a public stable after serving in World War II. His first stakes winner was Big If, who took the 1947 Remsen for two-year-old colts. His legacy, however, would be the extraordinary fillies he developed, including

Lamb Chop, the Champion Three-Year-Old of 1963, and Gamely, who won the 1967 Alabama Stakes at Saratoga and was the Champion Handicap Filly of 1968. Lamb Chop won 12 of 23 starts with five seconds and four thirds. Gamely had a record of 16 victories, nine seconds and six thirds in 41 starts. Chain Bracelet, Batteur, Desert Law, Discorama and Princessnesian were other major stakes winning fillies for Maloney, who tied for the 1970 Saratoga trainers title with Bobby Frankel with six victories.

Though he spent much of his career in New York, Maloney won the Santa Anita Derby and Strub Stakes twice each and saddled three consecutive winners of the Vanity Handicap in California.

Peter von Wiesenthal had horses with Maloney for 16 years. A graduate of Massachusetts Institute of Technology, von Wiesenthal spent his entire professional career in the processing industry, specializing in the field of combustion, and held several patents. He owned Alcorn Combustion Company with offices in New York, Philadelphia, London, Paris and Milan. Alcorn built parts for oil refineries and was the leading supplier of boiler-fired process heaters.

Von Wiesenthal and his wife, Ruth, an ex-rider herself better known as Bonnie, raced horses under Snowberry Farm, the name of their farm in Hudson, New York, that she still maintains, though her husband passed away in 1990. Becky Schroeder is Snowberry's farm manager.

The von Wiesenthals, who had purchased just one previous Thoroughbred without success, encountered Move It Now, a half-sister to six other winners including near $200,000-earner Three Martinis, at the Saratoga Yearling Sale in 1978. "There were two horses we liked, a colt and a filly," Bonnie von Wiesenthal said. "We went by the sale around 4:30 in the afternoon. Jim (Maloney) wanted to see something. He had them go open the top door of the colt's stall, and the colt left his food and came to the door. He did it again with the filly, and she didn't lift her head out of the feed bucket. He said, 'That's the one we'll bid on.'"

Their bid of $43,000 got the filly, and she was sent to Camden, South Carolina, to be broken. The following April, she was shipped north to the Maloney stable, and it didn't take anyone long too long to figure out she had a world of speed and ability. And she was not a secret when she made her two-year-old debut in the ninth race at Belmont Park, a maiden race for two-year-old New York-bred fillies, September 17, 1979. Sent off at odds of 3-2 from the eight post, she broke fifth, then quickly sped to the lead in a quick first quarter of a mile of :22 3/5. She was four lengths clear at that point, and widened her margin to 10 by running a half mile in :46 1/5. She cruised home in 1:11 1/5, 13 lengths ahead of the competition. "She was such a running machine," von Wiesenthal said.

Move It Now's debut was impressive enough to get a mention in Leo Waldman's New York column in the Daily Racing Form: "Ruth von Wiesenthal seems to have a promising two-year-old filly in Move It Now."

She made just one other start at two, finished second by three-quarters of a length to Sugar Dottie in an allowance race at Belmont 12 days after her debut victory.

Maloney and the von Wiesenthals were hoping for a big three-year-old season by Move It Now, and she did not disappoint them, winning her three-year-old debut, an allowance race for New York-bred fillies at Aqueduct, May 10, 1980, by 8 1/2 lengths over Adlibber in a sparkling 1:22 3/5 for seven furlongs.

Maloney was confident enough of Move It Now's class that he entered her against colts in the $50,000 Albany Handicap for three-year-old New York-breds. Move It Now won by a nose over Screenland.

Maloney upped the ante. He entered Move It Now in an open stakes race, the $40,000 Wistful for three-year-old fillies at Belmont Park, June 18th, and she finished fourth, 9 1/4 lengths behind Erin's Word.

After bouncing back to win an allowance race by five lengths in her first start on turf, Move It Now finished second in another grass allowance before returning to dirt, where she finished second by a length and a half to Adlibber in the $50,000 Mount Vernon Stakes at Belmont July 28th.

Maloney figured that set her up perfectly for another shot against males in the first $100,000 stakes for New York-breds, the DeWitt Clinton, at a mile and an eighth at Saratoga, the eighth of nine races on Wednesday, August 6th.

Hernandez and Maloney were confident, even after she drew a tough outside post, the 12, in a field of 12. The scratch of Adlibber would reduce the field to 11. "She would have won because of her speed," Hernandez said. "She was a really good filly."

Maloney agreed. "Jim was very confident that day," von Wiesenthal said. "He asked a few friends to come that day and he never did that."

George Cassidy, and his grand nephew, Marshall Cassidy, were about to do something they had been doing for years. George would push the button that would allow the DeWitt Clinton field to spring out of the starting gate, and Marshall would call the race on the public address system.

The Cassidy family has been affiliated with Thoroughbred racing for the better part of a century. Mars Cassidy, George's father, was born in 1862 in Elliott City, Maryland, and became a starter at the turn of the 20th Century for New York's racetracks for more than a quarter of a century.

The *Thoroughbred Record* (now the *Thoroughbred Times*) called Mars Cassidy "one of the most best known and liked figures on the American turf," following his death in October 1929.

When he was a young man, he owned a livery stable in Washington, D.C., and became a starter at Alexandria Island, Virginia, with no previous experience. He started horses at tracks in the Washington, D.C., area, then decided to train his own stable of horses, and was, at one point, affiliated with the legendary James "Sonny Jim" Fitzsimmons, a Hall of Fame trainer.

Cassidy, however, returned to being a starter, working at several tracks in Canada before moving on to New York, where he started his first race at Aqueduct in 1902. He worked at Aqueduct, Belmont Park, Coney Island, Empire City, Jamaica and Saratoga in New York, as well as at Hialeah in Miami, until his death, and was the first starter to regularly use a barrier of rubber rope that stretched across the track and would spring back to the fence when released.

Cassidy's three sons followed him into racing. Wendell, the oldest, worked in California, where he was the presiding judge at Hollywood Park until his death in 1959.

Middle son Marshall developed the first modern starting gate as well as the modern photo finish camera. He also introduced the film patrol for stewards to review concerning objections and inquiries, and, as the Executive Secretary of the Jockey Club, founded the annual Jockey Club Round Table meeting at Saratoga. Earlier in his life, he had punched cattle, fought professionally and then worked in a variety of positions at the track: entry clerk, clerk of the scales, patrol judge, starter, paddock judge, racing secretary, steward and director of racing before serving as the Jockey Club's Executive Secretary from 1941 through 1964.

George, the youngest of Mars' Cassidy's three sons, began working at the racetrack at an early age as an assistant starter for his dad. "He was told, originally, that he'd be in a temporary position," Brian Cassidy, one of George's three sons, said. "It was temporary for 63 years."

George remembered one night with his dad his entire life. It was a story he shared with Janet Barrett of the Thoroughbred Record. Mars Cassidy took his son to a cock fight one night and afterwards stopped at a bar on Long Island with several friends. "We lived in Brooklyn then, and they all got loaded there, so my father said, 'George, drive the car,'" George recounted. The car was a Cadillac and George was only 14 years old. After a while, Mars reconsidered the situation and took the steering wheel. "On Bedford Avenue, there was an iron horse with a general on it," George said. "And he ran straight into it. Now the car's all busted up." When the cops arrived, Mars knew all of them, which may be why he had the nerve to say, "That damn thing ran right in front of me."

Upon his father's death in 1929, George Cassidy took over as the starter at the New York tracks. He hadn't been in his new position long when he suffered one of his most anxious moments before the start of the 1930 Belmont Stakes as Gallant Fox and his jockey Earl Sande attempted to complete the Triple Crown at Belmont Park. "Earl Sande was turned sideways, awaiting the break, when he suddenly wheeled his horse to the tape, just as I sprung it," Cassidy said in the July, 1979, issue of The Backstretch magazine. "Sande got Gallant Fox off to a grand start and his horse led all the way, winning by three lengths. Gallant Fox hadn't gotten off well in the Kentucky Derby and Preakness, though he won them. I guess Sande was trying to give himself a better chance in the Belmont by taking an edge. He won, but I suspended him 10 days for his tactics. He might have been the last rider I set down."

But it wasn't the first time he suspended Sande, who had come out of retirement to ride Gallant Fox. In Barrett's Thoroughbred Record story, Cassidy recalled giving Sande 10 days previously. "He was supposed to ride in the Derby or something, and I gave him 10 days," Cassidy said. "That night, I went in the butcher shop in Queens Village. I'll never forget it. The butcher said to me, 'How 'bout that jerk that set Earl down!' He had a knife in his hand. I said to myself, 'I've got to get out of here. He'll chop me apart!'"

Actually, Cassidy was held in such esteem that he was shipped in from New York to Baltimore to start Seabiscuit and War Admiral's legendary 1937 match race because War Admiral's owner, Samuel Riddle, had a previous disagreement with the starter at Pimlico Race Course. "This was to be a walk-up start, and I was afraid," Cassidy said in The Backstretch article. "With a walk-up start, you must do it right the first time. There is no margin for error. Fortunately, the two horses were ridden by two top riders and they got them away perfectly."

Cassidy was the starter in the Belmont Stakes for 10 of the 11 Triple Crown winners in racing history, beginning with Gallant Fox in 1930 and stretching to Affirmed in 1978.

Cassidy got involved in the manufacturing of starting gates in the early 1940s after racing officials in New York asked if he could design a new gate. The existing gate had doors that locked and were opened when an electrical current was inserted into the lock. It did not always work because the battery wasn't 100 percent reliable. After conferring with an engineer at Bell Laboratory. Cassidy came up with a better idea: a gate with stall doors which were spring loaded and kept closed by electromagnets. So instead of using the current to open the stalls, Cassidy made the doors open simply by cutting off the electricity. "There's no way for it to fail," he told the Thoroughbred Record.

Cassidy started his own company, United Starting Gate, and his gates were widely used. Then the Puett Gate Company sued for patent infringement. The case was heard in Baltimore, and the decision, against United, was made while Cassidy was working as a starter at Hialeah. "The judge called me back to Baltimore on contempt of court," Cassidy told the Thoroughbred Record. "When I went to court, it was a quarter to two. We lost the suit; he fined me $4,000 and put me in jail with a marijuana distributor and an automobile thief." One of them asked, "What are you in here for?" Cassidy replied, "I don't know what I'm in here for."

Cassidy's lawyer got the $4,000 out of a bank, and Cassidy paid the fine and was released, but not until 5 p.m. that afternoon. The Jockey Club appealed the decision, and United won. Puett's owner, Arnold Grant, donated the company to Syracuse University as a tax write-off. Syracuse wasn't interested, and United bought it and went about manufacturing the improved starting gate for tracks around the country.

Despite his afternoon as an inmate in Baltimore, Cassidy, just like his dad, was very popular among horsemen, who respected his ability and professionalism. "He was well liked by everyone at the track," George's son Brian, a 58-year-old security worker who lives in Brooklyn, said. "I never heard anyone say a bad word about him. He had a great sense of humor and loved to tell stories."

Not this one.

The 11 three-year-old New York-breds contesting the $100,000 DeWitt Clinton Stakes at a mile and an eighth were, in post position order:

1. **Quintessential**, a colt trained by Johnny Campo and ridden by apprentice Frank Lovato, Jr.
2. **Royal Manner**, a colt ridden by Jeff Fell
3. **Without Words**, a colt trained by Billy Turner and ridden by Dave Borden
4. **Bold Igloo**, a colt ridden by Jorge Velasquez
5. **Right On Louie**, a gelding ridden by Anthony Garramone
6. **D. J.'s Nitecap**, a gelding ridden by Darrell McHargue
7. **Screenland**, a filly trained by Allen Jerkens and ridden by Jean-Luc Samyn
8. **Naskra's Breeze**, a colt trained by Phil Johnson and ridden by Mike Gonzalez
9. **Ace Personality**, a colt ridden by Steve Cauthen
10. **Wittles Lane**, a filly ridden by Eddie Maple, and
11. **Move It Now**

Quintessential, who had won the New York Derby at Finger Lakes in his prior start, was the 121 pound high weight, conceding three to 12 pounds to his opponents. Move It Now, the 5-2 second choice in the wagering to Screenland, carried 116 pounds.

Walking Move It Now toward the starting gate, Hernandez was chatting to Move It Now's assistant starter, who had Move It Now's shank in one hand to lead her in. But

Cassidy pushed the button with Move It Now behind the starting gate.

Neither the riders, the horses nor the assistant starters in each stall were prepared, though some were better off than others.

In the ensuing chaos, Bonnie von Wiesenthal is still thankful that Move It Now's assistant starter reacted immediately by turning her horse around. "I think we owe the life of that filly to the gateman," she said in 2003. "He turned her around 180 degrees when everyone else went. She would have run right into the gate if she saw those other horses going."

Not all the other horses got going. Without Words and Bold Igloo literally walked out of the starting gate. Jeff Fell, riding Royal Manner, said he was watching for Move It Now to walk into the gate when the race started. Jean-Luc Samyn, riding Screenland, said he was adjusting his goggles when the doors opened. "It's not fair," Samyn said afterwards. "They should cancel everything."

But the running of the DeWitt Clinton had continued with those horses who made it out of the starting gate. Riding Quintessential—even though his apprentice weight allowance of five pounds could not be used because this was a stakes race—Frank Lovato, Jr. did a masterful job. Quintessential survived an early speed duel with Royal Manner, then had enough left to hold off D. J.'s Nitecap by a neck. Screenland was another two lengths back in third. Without Words ran a remarkable race to finish fourth, 2 1/2 lengths behind Screenland. Ace Personality, Bold Igloo, Right On Louie, Royal Manner, Naskra's Breeze—who would go on to win a turf stakes at Saratoga—and Wittles Lane completed the order of finish.

Nobody was happier than Lovato, who still rides at the Fair Grounds in New Orleans and at Arlington Park in Chicago. "It was big for me because I was an apprentice," he said in December 2003. "It was my first stakes at Saratoga, and, I think, my first stakes win in New York."

Lovato's horse, Quintessential, had been the first to

load because he was on the rail. "I was just looking back to see how many horses were left behind the gate," Lovato said.

The gates opened before the last horse got in. "Fortunately, I had a handful of mane," Lovato said. "I thought it was an accident, that a horse broke through the gate. I really wasn't sure what happened. I just rode my race. It wasn't until I came back and heard all the yelling that I found out what happened. I was amazed."

Announcer Marshall Cassidy called the race as if nothing had happened, because he did not notice what had happened. "Did I see it?" he asked 23 years later. "No. Even though the horse left out was in green and white silks, I didn't see her. I went ahead and called the race. An announcer works from memory. You call what you see. When the stewards' phone rang and they told me there was an inquiry, I watched the video tape. I said, 'Oh, my God. George, what happened?'"

That question would be asked many times.

"I'll never forget it," Bonnie von Wiesenthal said. "I thought Jim Maloney was going to drop dead on the spot. We're sitting there. Jim Maloney stood there and turned bright red. He had a ruddy complexion anyway. He turned gray and then purple. I thought he was going to have a heart attack. I really did. I was terrified. Jim said, 'We've got to go to the steward's office.'"

Hernandez didn't know what to do. "I was really upset," he said. "I talked to Jim Maloney afterwards. He was as shocked as everybody. We kept saying, 'Can you believe this? Can you believe this?' I was just angry about it. I walked in the jockey's room. I had a whip in my hand. I hit the water cooler with the whip. It broke. I knew I broke something. Tony, the Clerk of Scales, told me, 'Ruben, calm down. There's nothing we can do about it.'"

Other people had to do something about it. Of immediate concern to the New York Racing Association was the outcome of the race. NYRA basically had three options: declare the race a no-contest for both betting and the distribution of purse money; let the race stand and refund all bets, or let the race stand and offer refunds to the horses it determined had not had a fair start.

As a crowd of 23,265 at Saratoga Race Course watched and waited to see what would happen, NYRA decided to let the race stand for purse money, while reserving the option of changing its distribution. NYRA declared Move It Now, Without Words and Bold Igloo non-starters and refunded all wagers involving them. More than $104,000 in win, place and show bets and an additional $47,918 in Late Doubles (on the eighth race, the DeWitt Clinton, and the ninth) were refunded on the three horses. Stewards ultimately decided to return the starting fees to the connections of Move It Now and Bold Igloo, but allow Without Words' fourth place finish to stand.

With the odds recalculated to not include the three non-starters, Screenland was the 6-5 favorite, with Quintessential 3-1 and Naskra's Breeze 4-1. The odds were lower than they had been when Move It Now was left behind the starting gate, but at least winning bettors got some of the money they had legitimately won.

Maloney was understandably livid after the race. "Big deal if the money is returned," he said. "There was no reason for this at all. This should be called a no contest. Obviously, I'm going to the stewards."

On the way to the stewards' office, Maloney and the von Wiesenthals heard cries from irate racing fans. "It's funny how the average bettor knows who you are," Bonnie von Wiesenthal said. "They said, 'You'll sue. You'll sue.' Of course we wouldn't."

But they did want justice. And that meant another shot at the same stakes race at the same track. But they did not get to meet with NYRA Chairman of the Board Ogden Mills "Dinny" Phipps and President Gerard McKeon until the following morning.

In the interim, George Cassidy took the entire blame immediately after the race. "I didn't see Move It Now behind the gate," he said. "He (sic) was between some lead ponies and

I didn't see him (sic). I hit the start button. I should have counted all the horses before the start. It was all my fault."

And he heard about it as he walked to the stewards' office. "Of course, the crowd was getting on him," George Cassidy's son, Brian, said. "One guy yelled, 'Hey, Cassidy, you couldn't find your way to the 'D' train.' My dad yelled back, 'I couldn't even find the 'D' train.' He had a good sense of humor."

Obscured by all this was the fine ride Lovato had given Quintessential. "Let me tell you this . . . Frank is a super rider," trainer Johnny Campo said. "For me to use a bug rider (apprentice) in a stakes race is saying something."

What could be said about Move It Now?

The following morning, Peter and Bonnie von Wiesenthal and Jim Maloney met with Phipps and McKeon. Bonnie recounted what followed:

> "Dinny started out by saying, 'I know how you're feeling. I'm a breeder also. I know what it would have meant to your filly.'
>
> "When he stopped, my husband spoke. He was a gentleman. He was not an aggressive type of person. He was very quiet. He said, 'You know, Dinny, I build the hot end of oil refineries and chemical plants around the world. If I build something to sell, and there's something wrong, do you know what they say to me? What are you going to do about it?'
>
> "Jim (Maloney) had told us they would offer another race at Belmont. He wanted another race at Saratoga.
>
> "Dinny said, 'I have to see what the money is.'
>
> "My husband said, 'I want an identical race at Saratoga around two turns.'
>
> "Dinny said, 'I have to see. I have to see. We'll meet next afternoon at 2.'"

The next day, Phipps had good news for Move It Now's connections. In an unprecedented move, NYRA announced that there would be an identical race for three-year-old New York-breds named the West Point Handicap, at the same mile and an eighth distance with the same $100,000 purse on August 25th.

"In fairness to all concerned, Mr. Van Lindt (John Van Lindt, Chairman of the New York State Racing and Wagering Board and a member of the New York State Thoroughbred Breeders' Fund Board) and I decided that another mile and an eighth event for New York-breds should be scheduled before the Saratoga meet ends," Phipps said. "In this manner, I feel the NYRA will have done its best to rectify he unfortunate incident for both horsemen and the fans."

In the following morning's *Times Union* newspaper, Sports Editor Tom Cunningham went to bat for Cassidy, saying, "If George Cassidy had become an accountant and made the same number of mistakes he made as starter of horses for the New York Racing Association over the past 51 years, he'd be still using his first eraser." Noting that Cassidy had started some 125,000 races in his distinguished career, he concluded, "He has sent the great horses of the past half-century on their way and has done it with distinction and ability. But at this time, George Cassidy is feeling mighty low. He can't forgive himself for that second goof in 51 years. George, you haven't even put a dent in the eraser."

In a perfect world, Move It Now would have won the re-scheduled stakes, Cassidy would have been forgiven and everybody could have turned the page. That didn't happen.

While training for the West Point Handicap, Move It Now suffered an injury. "That filly was so fit to run that he (Maloney) had to work her two days later," Bonnie von Wiesenthal said. "We were at a cocktail party that night, and Jim came up to me and said, 'You have a job to do, Bonnie. When I worked the filly, she hurt her ankle. You have to write Dinny, telling him, thanks for the race, but we can't run.'"

She did exactly that. "I thought that was the right thing to do," she said.

Unfortunately, Move It Now's injury was more serious than originally suspected, and she missed the rest of her three-year-old season. At four in 1981, she finished third and first in two allowance races on grass, third in the Kingston Stakes on turf behind Adlibber and Without Words and second in an allowance race before winning the Mount Vernon Stakes on grass by a head over Adlibber.

Ironically, Move It Now made her final career start in the West Point Handicap at Saratoga, which had been moved to turf for its second running, August 21, 1981. Move It Now finished fourth by three lengths in the field of 12 to Naskra's Breeze.

Move It Now retired with a career record of six wins, four seconds, two thirds and two fourths in 14 career starts, and earnings of $184,323.

She was purchased back to be a broodmare by John Hettinger at Keeneland for $40,000, three thousand less than he had sold her for as a yearling. "For us, it was wonderful because we knew she'd have a good home," Bonnie von Wiesenthal said.

She did, enjoying modest success as a broodmare. "She had a good life here," Hettinger said. "We all loved her."

The re-running of the DeWitt Clinton as the West Point turned out to be a windfall for Quintessential's connections, owner Charles Petigrow, trainer Campo and jockey Lovato, and for anyone who bet on the colt.

The West Point field was less challenging than the DeWitt Clinton. Besides Move It Now's absence, Screenland was a late scratch. Then, in the post parade, D. J.'s Nitecap, the third betting choice in the West Point because of his fast finishing second in the DeWitt Clinton, got loose and ran off. He was finally apprehended and scratched. Two other of Quintessential's opponents, Anonymous Prince and Cassie's Birthday, were, ironically, left in the gate after a normal start.

But Quintessential, who had been 3-1 when he won as the high weight in the DeWitt Clinton, opened at 18-1 in the wagering for the West Point and went off at 5-1, perhaps because he was carrying an additional five pounds, spotting his rivals nine to 17 pounds. Adlibber, who had been scratched before the DeWitt Clinton, went off the 7-5 favorite under Angel Cordero, Jr. Winter Words was the 5-2 second choice.

Quintessential stalked 80-1 longshot Right Approach down the backstretch and around the far turn, collared him in upper stretch and aired by 4 1/4 lengths over Winter Words, who rallied to finish second. Right Approach was third, a half length behind Winter Words and five in front of Adlibber. "They didn't bet on me again," Lovato said. "My horse won even easier."

Thus did Quintessential become the first horse in Saratoga's storied history to win two $100,000 races in one meet. Alydar nearly did in 1977 when he won the Whitney and the Travers, but the Whitney was not worth $100,000 then.

Off three consecutive stakes victories, Quintessential never won another race. He finished his three-year-old season with one third in four starts; posted one third in four starts as a four-year-old in 1981, and finished ninth by 17 lengths and fourth by 15 lengths in his only two starts at five in 1982.

He had made $159,135 in winning the 1980 New York Derby, DeWitt Clinton and West Point in the space of five weeks. In his final 10 starts over the next two years he made $16,758. Talk about being in the right place at the right time.

Announcer Marshall Cassidy said he never spoke to his grand-uncle George about Move It Now's race. "I felt so bad for him," Marshall said. "I empathized with him."

George Cassidy was forced into retirement by the New York Racing Association. "I think he worked until the end of 1980," his son, Brian, said. "What happened was they called my father and said, 'George, we think it's a good time for you to step down.'"

Cassidy did so reluctantly. "He didn't want to retire," Brian said. "He was kind of hurt by it. He did a lot for racing.

His family did a lot for racing. The next thing you know, they call him up and said, 'We want you out of there.'"

It was an inglorious conclusion to a distinguished career. Maybe John Hettinger said it best: "He was a great man and a good starter. And we all make mistakes."

Angel Cordero, Jr.
Retirement Ceremony, 1992
(*Photo Courtesy of Barbara D. Livingston*)

CHAPTER 5

Angel

Angel Cordero, Jr., arrived in Saratoga Springs unknown and nearly broke in August 1962, a 19-year-old kid from Puerto Rico desperate for a chance to ride horses. "I was galloping horses for free," he said.

He had just won his first race in New York on Counterrate, July 26th at Aqueduct. Nobody noticed. And, certainly, no trainer was inclined to give him a mount at Saratoga Race Course's prestigious meet. "I always had problems at Saratoga in the beginning of my career," Cordero said. "In 1962, I stayed one week, galloping horses. In 1963, one week. I had to go home. I didn't have any money."

"Home" was his sister's apartment in the projects of Manhattan. "I stayed with my sister for two years," Cordero said. "I used to get on horses with the same clothes I brought from Puerto Rico. People said, 'Look at that kid. He's tough.' I didn't have anything else to wear."

A year later, he was so frustrated with his lack of success at New York's major tracks that he headed to Finger Lakes. He'd been given a letter of recommendation to bring to trainers there. Cordero trekked up to central New York State and accomplished nothing. "I went to Finger Lakes for nine days and didn't get a single ride there," he said.

He returned to New York, where he was living with

jockey Eddie Belmonte and his family, and decided he would head back to Puerto Rico to stay. "Eddie saw me packing my clothes," Cordero said. "He said, 'Maybe you should go. New York is for good jockeys only.' That hit me." He thought back to what his father had once told him in Puerto Rico, where Cordero's father, grandfather and uncles were jockeys. Cordero said he wanted to be like one of his uncles, one who was very successful: "My father said, 'You'll never be like him. You'll never be like your uncles,'" Cordero said. "That put some fire in me."

Cordero unpacked his bags. Then he went to Saratoga to become a legend.

He rode his first horse at Saratoga in the first race of opening day, Monday, August 2, 1965, finishing third on a 40-1 longshot named Arranger. Three days later, Cordero found the Saratoga winner's circle when Gator Ray won the second race, a six furlong sprint for claimers, easily at 3-1.

Two years later, Cordero won his first Saratoga riding title. Belmonte was a distant second.

Cordero didn't win another title until 1976. Then he forgot how to lose at Saratoga.

Even more amazing than Cordero's 11 consecutive riding titles from 1976 to 1986 were the obstacles he overcame to win them. Twice, he lost crucial days because of suspensions, yet still won the 24-day meet. Twice Cordero got dumped in a turf race when his horse veered through the hedges coming out of the far turn, and he still won two titles. One year, he won despite a zero-for-22 slump. He won another despite going two-for-47 and nearly being trampled to death in one of the most terrifying spills in modern Saratoga history. Cordero was back riding 24 hours later.

When Jose Santos finally unseated Cordero in 1987, Cordero responded by winning two more titles in 1988 and 1989. Thirteen titles in 14 years.

"I wanted to be the best," Cordero said.

And he was.

At Saratoga, through the 2003 meet. Cordero's 640

career wins ranked him first in modern Saratoga racing history, according to the National Museum of Racing and Hall of Fame, which totaled jockeys records from 1940 to the present. Jerry Bailey, who won four consecutive titles from 1994-1997 and three more from 1999-2001, was second with 618. No other jockey reached 400.

Though he stood an excellent chance of passing Cordero's total in the 2004 meet, Bailey's admiration of Cordero is unabashed. "He was a brilliant rider," Bailey said. "I don't care how many I won in a row. I would never approach what he did."

To accomplish what he did, Cordero rode through 23 major accidents before the 24th finally forced him to retire in 1992. "I wanted it so bad," he said. "I rode with a lot of pain and broken bones. Stupid things you do when you're young. I made it the hard way, and I paid the price."

At Saratoga, it always seemed worth it. But his Saratoga success did not happen overnight.

Though Cordero learned much from his family in Puerto Rico, where he rode his first winner, Celador, at El Commandante Racetrack on June 15, 1960, at the age of 17, the jockey he emulated when he came to the United States was Eddie Arcaro. "I thought Arcaro was the best I ever saw," Cordero said. "Because he rode in the 1940s, the 1950s and the 1960s. He was the quickest at changing hands. There was nobody close to him. We all learn from somebody. I learned from him. My father taught me a lot and my grandfather and uncles, but I watched Arcaro on film and tried to imitate him. If you're a boxer, you imitate Ali. If you play baseball, you imitate Willie Mays. You imitate and then you develop your own style."

Cordero's style was doing anything he could to win a race, from serenading skittish horses in Spanish on the way to the post parade to testing the limits of every rule of racing. Through 1989, his 248 suspensions were three times higher than any other active jockey. Yet a dozen years after his retirement in 1992, he remains one of just seven jockeys to win 7,000 races in his career.

The 1974 Kentucky Derby demonstrated Cordero's brilliance. Hall of Fame trainer Woody Stephens, immortalized by his five consecutive Belmont Stakes victories from 1982 through 1986, rarely used Cordero. Eddie Maple was Stephens' main man, and, when he was unavailable, Stephens usually turned to Laffit Pincay, Jr., or Chris McCarron. In the 1974 Derby, though, Stephens tabbed Pincay and Cordero to ride his two horse entry, Pincay on Judger, considered the better of the two, and Cordero on Cannonade. Because there was no clear leader of the three-year-old division that spring, a field of 23 entered the 100th Kentucky Derby, so unmanageable a quantity of horses that the Derby field would be restricted to 20 the very next year.

Judger finished eighth. "Things didn't break for him in the Derby," Stephens said. "Judger had the 22 post and got in trouble."

Cannonade won, as Cordero weaved his way through unending traffic to get his first Kentucky Derby. "I never saw a horse get a better ride," Stephens said. "There's 23 horses. He (Cordero) kept sneaking through horses, outside and inside. Then, just before they turned for home, he switched to the outside because he thought if there was a challenge, it'd be from the outside. He wanted to be sure my horse would see another horse if a challenge came, but at the quarter pole he opened up three lengths and won easily. I thought that day, Cordero rode that horse as good as any I've ever seen."

Cordero's uncanny understanding of how a race would unfold was the product of spending as much as four hours a night handicapping every race he was in the following day. "It's like homework," he said in 1980. "Sometimes, I am up until two or three in the morning. I go home at night, put checks by the horses I have to beat. I mark speed horses. I check workouts. I figure out what I have to do the next day. I check out the trainers and the jockeys on horses that I have to beat."

One thing he couldn't beat was the prejudice he encountered early in his career as a dark skinned, Puerto Rican without connections. "People said, 'You're black. You're Spanish. You don't have a stable (contract). You'll never make it,'" Cordero said. Yet even after he had made it, his presence was sometimes unwelcome. "I rented a house in California one year," Cordero said. "They found out I'm Spanish and sent my money back to me."

California was where he had one of his worst accidents. Riding at Hollywood Park, Cordero went down in a race, April 26, 1978, and almost never got up. "It was just before Derby time," he said. "I broke my back. I compressed nine, 10 or 11 vertebrae. It was very serious, very scary."

It did not affect him when he came back. If there was a narrow opening between horses, Cordero took it, almost instinctively. He was absolutely fearless on the racetrack. "I think that's something born in every top athlete," Cordero said. "You can't have fear in boxing or baseball or basketball. Whatever sport you play, you can't be intimidated. I wasn't worried about getting hurt because I always came back."

Even after surgery. In a race on March 8, 1986, at Aqueduct, Cordero's horse, Highfalutin, clipped heels with another horse, and sent Cordero hurtling to the track. Cordero underwent four and a half hours of surgery to mend a lacerated liver and a fractured tibia. Cordero returned to the races four months later, winning on his only two mounts at Belmont Park, I'm Your Boy and the top two-year-old, Gulch—the horse he would win the Breeders' Cup Sprint with two and a half years later—in the Tremont Stakes, July 13th. Soon afterward, Cordero headed north to his favorite track, Saratoga, hoping to capture an unprecedented 11th consecutive riding title.

"The atmosphere at Saratoga really helps your attitude," he said at the time. "All year in New York, I go from my house to the track and from the track to my house. And like a horse, you get kind of sour. When you move to Saratoga, it inspires you, and you work a little harder. In Saratoga, people know I know the track and I ride a lot of winners there. So even people who don't ride me at Belmont give me a mount there. I've been coming to Saratoga since 1965. That has to be an advantage. I'm older than a lot of riders, so I do know the track better, and I work the horses in the morning at Saratoga, which helps me with the trainers. Saratoga is a good track, but it's a funny track. I remember, from 1965 to 1970, the rail was very heavy. Nobody wanted to be near it. Then it changed. The track looks one way in the morning, a different way in the afternoon. When it rains, you have to guess what part of the track is good." Cordero rarely guessed. Year after year, he seemed to be the first jockey to know if the rail was alive or dead, if speed was holding up or dying.

"Saratoga gives me great self-satisfaction," Cordero said. "I look forward to going to Saratoga every year and being the leading rider. The rest of the year, when I ride in New York at Belmont and Aqueduct, I try to win but I don't worry about being the leading rider. If I feel I can take a day off, I'll just do it. In the mornings, I go whenever I feel like riding workouts. But when I'm at Saratoga, I go every morning. I want to ride a lot of horses that can win."

At Saratoga, no jockey won more. And all of Cordero's titles came in a 24-day Saratoga meet, which was expanded to 30 days in 1991, 34 days in 1994 and its present 36 days in 1997.

Cordero's first Saratoga riding title was a runaway in 1967. His 35 victories from 171 mounts were 13 more than his benefactor, Belmonte, in second, and just six short of Manny Ycaza's record of 41 set in 1959.

Cordero didn't win another riding title for nine years. Jorge Velasquez won three in 1970, 1972 and 1974 with totals of 34, 20 and 20, respectively. Braulio Baeza (26), Jacinto Vasquez (22), Laffit Pincay, Jr. (25), Ron Turcotte (27) and Eddie Maple, who took the 1975 title with 23 victories, beat out Cordero the other years before Cordero's 11-year reign began in 1976 with 29 winners.

After winning titles in 1977 and 1978 with identical totals of 34, Cordero handicapped himself in 1979 by drawing a five-day suspension. Cordero was suspended for his ride on Lady Hardwick, the 3-5 favorite in a two-year-old maiden race on the inner turf course. Lady Hardwick won by a nose, but was disqualified and placed second. Despite missing five crucial days in the short 24-day meet, Cordero won his fourth straight title with 23 victories.

In 1980, Cordero made it five straight with 35 winners. Earlier that year, Cordero was involved in one of the most controversial races in the history of the Triple Crown. Riding Codex for trainer D. Wayne Lukas in the Preakness Stakes, Cordero took his horse extremely wide on far the turn just as the 1980 Kentucky Derby winning filly Genuine Risk was making her move under Vasquez. They appeared to bump before Codex drew off to a 4 3/4 length victory. There was an objection, but no disqualification, leaving an army of Genuine Risk fans bitter to this day believing Cordero had denied her the opportunity of becoming the first filly Triple Crown winner. It would not have happened anyway, as she ran a gallant second by two lengths to 53-to-1 longshot Temperence Hill in the Belmont Stakes on a muddy track. But her comment from the Daily Racing Form from the Preakness—as it appears in the Form's book "Champions"—is "Bothered (on the) turn."

Cordero wasn't bothered by the infamy. He was used to it. Fans and bettors hated when Cordero got away with his aggressive riding without punishment, unless they had bet on him. In the final yards of a tight finish, there was no one better than Cordero at getting every last ounce of effort from his horse. Never was that more evident than in the 1976 Belmont Stakes. Riding for Hall of Fame trainer Laz Barrera, Cordero had won the Kentucky Derby wire-to-wire with a Puerto Rican speedster named Bold Forbes. In that year's Preakness, however, Bold Forbes got hooked by the beaten favorite in the Derby, Honest Pleasure, in a suicidal speed duel that set up the race for a longshot named Elocutionist. People wondered how Bold Forbes could possibly make the mile and a half distance of the Belmont Stakes, but the horse had two Hall of Famers, Barrera and Cordero, as allies.

Barrera did a masterful job of training, and Cordero was at his absolute best. He nursed Bold Forbes on the lead and then spurted to a six length advantage at the head of the stretch. But as he traveled down the long Belmont Park stretch, Bold Forbes tired and began to bear out. Relentlessly driving his horse, Cordero kept him going straight enough to hold off McKenzie Bridge by a neck. "If you ride a horse that wins by 15 lengths, you haven't accomplished anything," Cordero said. "Anybody can win that. It's when you win a race that you contributed to winning that makes you feel good. On horses that, if you don't give them a good ride, they don't win. That makes you happy."

And Cordero was happiest at Saratoga. But in 1981, he was pushed to the limit by Eddie Maple and a 17-year-old apprentice whiz named Richard "The Mig" Migliore. The son of a Long Island banker, Migliore had rocketed to success in his first year of riding, winning the 1981 Aqueduct spring meet and finishing second to Cordero in the 1981 Belmont summer meet.

Heading into the next-to-last day of the 1981 Saratoga meet, Cordero, despite missing three days of the meet on a suspension and a lengthening slump he was still battling, held a narrow lead with 22 wins, one more than both Maple and Migliore. But Cordero was out of town the next-to-last afternoon, winning the Delaware Handicap on Relaxing and giving Maple and Migliore a great opportunity to make up ground. Neither did.

Migliore had already won his first $100,000 stakes with Accipiter's Hope and broken Steve Cauthen's apprentice record for earnings in a single season in less than eight months. In the third race that Sunday afternoon, August 24th, Migliore was on Crème De La Fete, a horse he'd won on three weeks earlier in the meet. Coming around the far turn, Migliore was moving Crème De La Fete up on the outside of the horse in first, Tantivy, when Tantivy suddenly bolted to the outside. Crème De La Fete went tumbling down over him, and then Big Greg, on the outside of those two horses, fell, sending his jockey, Ruben Hernandez, somersaulting to the track. Both jockeys escaped serious injury, though Migliore suffered a neck strain and abrasions on his wrist. Doctors feared he had a concussion and kept him in the hospital overnight, officially ending his Saratoga season. "I thought I was going to win the race," Migliore said afterwards. "I hadn't even asked my horse to run yet."

He would keep pleasant memories of Saratoga despite the injury. "It's been a great meet for me anyway," he said. "I won my first hundred grander and broke Cauthen's record up here. It was really terrific in Saratoga."

With Migliore out of the picture, the jockey title would be won by either Maple or Cordero. Both were enduring wicked slumps. Maple, who did not win a race on August 24th, ended his zero-for-23 string on closing day the following afternoon, capturing the seventh race on Novel Notion for his 22nd winner, tying Cordero for the lead. Cordero finished second in the seventh race with Lines of Power, extending his oh-fer to zero-for-22.

Both jockeys had longshot mounts in the ninth and last race—neither would finish in the money. So the title came down to a single race, the eighth, the mile and five-eighths $58,400 Seneca Handicap, a marathon turf race.

Making the race even sweeter was that Maple was riding Native Courier, who had won the 1979 Seneca Handicap, while Cordero was on Great Neck, who had won the 1980 Seneca. In 1981, Native Courier won one division of another Saratoga grass stakes race, the Bernard Baruch Handicap. Great Neck won the other.

Carrying high weight of 123 pounds, the five-year-old Great Neck, who had won his last two starts and just been purchased from John Nerud's Tartan Stable by Franklin Delano Roosevelt, Jr. for a reported $2.5 million, was sent off as the 6-5 favorite. The seven-year-old Native Courier, carrying 117, was the 7-2 second choice.

In the post parade, another starter in the Seneca, Wicked Will, reared and kicked Cordero. "It hurt like hell," Cordero said. "But no way I was getting off this horse."

Maple went for the lead right at the start and tried going wire-to-wire. Cordero secured a good spot on the rail and kept Great Neck there, alternating with Peat Moss, then Wicked Will, for second and third.

Taking advantage of no immediate pressure, Maple set slow fractions over a course labeled "good" after a brief thunderstorm earlier in the day had been followed by brilliant sunshine. Native Courier took the field of nine to the half in :51 2/5 and the mile in 1:40 1/5. "They were walking," Cordero said.

Nearing the final turn, the Seneca became a two horse race. Cordero moved Great Neck up to the outside of Native Courier, getting within half a length before Native Courier responded by surging to a full length advantage. Cordero thought he was done. "I didn't think I was going to win at the head of the stretch," he said. "I thought, 'What a way to lose. I'm going to wind up empty without 23."

But Cordero got his 23rd. Great Neck merely needed time to get rolling with his weight. He caught Native Courier by the sixteenth pole and increased his lead with every step to win by three lengths in 2:40 4/5, 3 3/5 seconds slower than his winning time the year before.

Cordero had his sixth straight Saratoga title. "It feels great," he said after the Seneca. "You're psyched for the whole year. You work all month. And it comes down to one race."

He extended the streak to eight with 30 winners in 1982 and 31 in 1983. He led the nation in earnings both years and was honored with his only two Eclipse Awards as Outstanding Jockey. He was at the apex of his career. Until he went down in another horrifying accident. This one was at Saratoga. "The ugliest accident I ever had," Cordero said 19 years later. "I got run over by two horses."

If ever there was a year Cordero should have been beaten at Saratoga, it was in 1984, when one of his mounts, A Phenomenon, a horse he'd won the Jim Dandy Stakes on the previous year, died on the track in the middle of a stakes race. Owned by Brownell Combs II and trained by Angel Penna, Jr., A Phenonmenon took a career record of six wins, three seconds and a third in 11 starts into the starting gate as the prohibitive

2-5 favorite in a field of six contesting the $88,590 Forego Handicap, a seven furlong stakes named for the three-time Horse of the Year, on Sunday, August 20th.

Cordero was leading the rider standings with 16 victories despite another horrendous slump. He had lost 11 straight and 33 of his last 35 mounts before the Forego. Then he nearly lost his life.

A Phenomenon had out-dueled Mugatea, ridden by Robbie Davis, for the early lead and was in front midway into the final turn when he broke down, suffering what a track spokesman later said was an irreparable compound fracture of the left pastern and cannon bone.

"His horse broke down on the inside," Davis said. "Angel tried holding him up to keep the horse from going down."

Grabbing the reins of A Phenomenon and trying to maintain his balance, Cordero was suspended in mid-air for an instant, his left leg dangling over A Phenomenon. Then Cordero was spun around and dumped to the track, still holding the reins in his right hand, as A Phenomenon went down. A Phenomenon was later humanely euthanized.

Cordero's fall left him immediately in the path of one horse, Vittorioso, ridden by Don MacBeth. Vittorioso seemed to run over Cordero's body. Then another horse, Shadowmar, came close to trampling Cordero.

"You just go down," Cordero said the next day. "You don't know what's behind you. I looked at the film later. I couldn't believe it. When I went down, I thought I was gone. I thought both horses were going to hit me. Somebody up there must like me. Not too many do."

The 41-year-old Cordero was rushed by ambulance to Saratoga Hospital and was released. He had, miraculously, avoided serious injury, suffering only a bruised lower back.

Cordero was back to ride the next day. "The doctor said I might have internal bleeding," Cordero said. "He said, 'If you go to the bathroom and have blood, call me.' I had blood that night and the next morning, but I was scared and didn't go back. I had the mark of a horseshoe in my tailbone."

Yet he rode the next day. "I've been riding for 24 years," Cordero said at the time. "When you get hurt, your muscles are sore. It doesn't do you any good to sit home. I'm used to pain. It's nothing new to me. As long as nothing is broken . . . eight of 10 athletes have pain."

He was back riding, but his slump continued. Eddie Maple took the lead in the jockey standings with his 17th winner on Wednesday, August 23rd, the 20th day of the 24-day meet. The 35-year-old Maple had won the 1975 Saratoga meet with 23 winners before Cordero began his streak. Surprisingly, despite being one of just eight riders with more than $40 million in career earnings at the time, Maple had won just one other riding title in New York, at Aqueduct 1976. At Saratoga in 1983, Maple won 13 races, 18 less than Cordero. In 1984, he had the opportunity to beat him.

"Listen, I'm the challenger," he said after taking the lead that Wednesday. "I would be very happy to win it, and I'm going to try and win it. It would be nice. I'm certainly going to try my hardest."

A win early on the Thursday card gave Maple an 18-16 lead before Cordero finally broke loose. He had lost 21 straight, with only two wins in his last 47 mounts, when he guided Coyote Dancer to a 4 1/4 length romp in the sixth race at odds of 5-2. Then Maple won another race that day, taking the Seneca Handicap (which had been moved from closing day the previous year) by a fraction of a nose on Persian Tiara.

There were three days left in the meet, and Maple led 19-17.

Maple had two winners in the next two days. Cordero had four. That made it 21-all.

This time, Maple missed the final Sunday of the meet, journeying to Chicago to ride Majesty's Prince in the Budweiser Arlington Million at Arlington Park. Majesty's Prince finished sixth to John Henry.

Cordero spent Sunday winning two maiden races at Saratoga on Lady Marinat ($10.20) and first-time starter Climb The Heights ($7.60). In the featured $122,400 Hopeful Stakes that afternoon, Cordero finished fifth on Vindaloo to Chief's Crown, ridden by MacBeth. Voted Two-Year-Old Champion after winning the first Breeders' Cup race ever, the 1984 Juvenile at Hollywood Park, Chief's Crown would return to Saratoga at three, giving Cordero two memorable trips as he temporarily subbed for MacBeth. In the Tell Stakes, his first start on turf, Chief's Crown won by three-quarters of a length, but was disqualified and placed fourth for coming out on the final turn. Chief's Crown made it up to Cordero in his next start, winning the Travers by 2 1/4 lengths. It would be Cordero's lone Travers victory in 19 tries.

Cordero entered closing day that Monday with a 23-21 lead on Maple. Maple, though, won the first race on Crowning ($15.60). Neither jockey won races two through seven. But in the eighth, the $119,800 Spinaway Stakes for two-year-old fillies, Cordero rode Tiltalating, the even money favorite. Maple rode Contradance, who spotted the field at least a dozen lengths when she stumbled leaving the starting gate. Tiltalating won by a length and a quarter. Contradance rallied to finish third. Cordero beat Maple 24-22. He had done it again, his ninth consecutive title. "This is one of my hardest years," he said after the Spinaway. "I'm very happy. I feel 10 years younger."

Cordero won his 10th straight in 1985, finishing with 22 winners, three more than Jean Cruguet in second. "It meant a lot to me to win for 10 years," Cordero said on closing day. "It's a lot of pressure when you are going for something special like that. All the things I have accomplished, all the records . . . it's something that'll be there for a long time."

The following spring, Cordero went down again at Aqueduct.

Who would give him a chance to win an 11th straight coming off his frightening accident on Highfalutin on March 8, 1986? He'd been out of action for more than four months when he made his triumphant return, winning two races at Belmont Park that July 13th. Saratoga would open just 18 days later, leaving the 43-year-old Cordero precious little time to regain his conditioning. Cordero's stranglehold on Saratoga seemed ready to sunset. And the rider most likely to beat him was 18 years younger. Jose Santos, who began riding at Hipico Racecourse in his native Chile at the age of 14, moved to Florida in 1984, winning riding titles at Calder, Gulfstream and Hialeah. Santos moved to New York in mid-1985 and quickly established himself, finishing third in his first Saratoga meeting. He won the 1986 Belmont Park summer meet and seemed poised to dethrone Cordero at Saratoga that August.

Cordero, though, wasn't ready to lose his grip on the Saratoga riding title. So he came out every morning at Saratoga and rode workouts, then came back each afternoon and rode seven, eight or even nine races a day. "I worked so hard," he told Albany *Times Union*'s Tim Wilkin. "You don't know how important this was to me."

Cordero dominated the first half of the meet, but then slowed down. "As the meet went on, I found myself getting more tired," he said. "Not as much physically, but mentally."

His nine win lead on Santos was cut to two heading into closing day as Cordero finished the meet four-for-34. The fourth winner was in the third race closing day on the three-year-old filly Once And For All. That clinched his 11th straight title. Santos finished second twice, without winning. When Santos failed to win the seventh, Cordero was given a crown and a cape from the New York Racing Association. He was king again with 27 winners, three ahead of Santos. Velasquez was a distant third with 16. Cordero celebrated by drinking a Miller Lite in the jockey's room. "I've never finished this poorly up here," he told Wilkin. "I would have been very disappointed if I hadn't got it. It really would have been bad for my mind. This would have been the first time in my career that I hadn't gotten something that I had aimed for."

Santos took the close second with class. "I thought I

had a shot," he said. "I did the best I could, but Angel, he is the king of the riders, especially up here."

The next year, Santos took him down.

Cordero and Santos were close in the 1987 rider standings until the third week, when Cordero went through a zero-for-25 draught, a slump even Cordero could not recover from. Santos finished with 26 winners, four more than Cordero, and Saratoga had a new leading rider for the first time in more than a decade. "As long as I have been coming up to Saratoga, I can't ever remember having a slump like that," Cordero told Wilkin. "He was winning races. I wasn't. There were an awful lot of horses I had that finished second (23). It was like having the bases loaded with no outs and not being able to score. It was frustrating. I'm not happy that I lost this, but I'm not real upset. I'm not going to go home and cry or hang myself from a tree. You have to give credit to Jose. He had a great meet. I'm not ashamed of being beat by him. I would be ashamed if I got beat by someone who couldn't ride."

Santos certainly could. He had led the country in earnings in 1986 and would do it again in 1987, in 1988 when he won his lone Eclipse Award, and in 1989. He would win the 2002 $4 million Breeders' Cup Classic on 43-1 longshot Volponi for trainer Phil Johnson and add the 2003 Kentucky Derby and Preakness on Funny Cide.

But unseating Cordero at Saratoga in 1986 was a major coup, and Santos fully appreciated it. "To beat a rider like Angel Cordero is an accomplishment," he said on closing day. "I worked hard for this and I'm glad I won. For the first time in a long time, he'll be coming up here next year looking for revenge."

He'd get it, easily, despite battling chicken pox and stomach cramps earlier in the summer of 1988. At Saratoga, Cordero had to have his blood checked out periodically because he was getting exhausted riding workouts every morning and any mount he could get each afternoon, the price he paid to return to the top of the Saratoga standings at the age of 45. "I felt a lot of pressure coming in," Cordero told Wilkin.

"I didn't want to come back to Saratoga and get beat again. To be very honest with you, I don't know if I could have dealt with that."

The timing would have been terrible. Cordero was inducted that August into the National Museum of Racing's Hall of Fame on Union Avenue across the street from the main entrance of Saratoga Race Course.

Cordero won the 1988 Saratoga meet with 36 wins from 141 mounts, an extraordinary win percentage of 25.5 at the nation's toughest meet. Santos and Pat Day tied for second with 27.

Still, with his highest total of Saratoga winners in his entire career, Cordero had come up five short of Ycaza's record, the one Saratoga jewel to elude him. "I don't know how the hell Manny did it," Cordero said.

Cordero had done enough. "People always talk about age," he said. "All I wanted to do in Saratoga was prove a point, to show everyone. If I was younger and got the title back, no one would think of it as a big deal. I did it when I was 45. I am proud."

And he was spent. "I feel like I'm 80," he said on closing day. "I'm dying to go back home because I'm mentally and physically beat up."

He recovered well enough to win the Saratoga title again the next year with 34 wins, his 13th title in 14 years. He had won 404 races in those 14 years, a healthy slice of his 7,057 career victories.

Cordero finished second to Chris Antley at Saratoga in 1990. In 1991, he was in a great battle for the title with Mike Smith and Julie Krone. The meet had been extended to 30 days that summer, and when Cordero won the second race on Saturday, August 28th by a neck on a New York-bred named Fabersham at odds of 5-2 for trainer Tom Skiffington, Jr., he moved one up on Smith, who, ironically, had taken off Fabersham to ride Way Of The Barron, who finished a well beaten fourth as the 8-5 favorite.

Fabersham was Cordero's last Saratoga winner. He

ended the meet zero-for-18, finishing third with 30 victories. Smith won the title with 33, one more than Krone.

Angel Cordero, Jr.'s last ride at Saratoga was in the ninth race on closing day, Monday, August 26th, on Believe My Curves. Sent off at 5-1 in the field of 11 New York-bred maiden fillies, Believe My Curves finished sixth by 6 1/4 lengths. Krone rode the winner, Winter Affair, who scored by a neck at 5-2.

On January 12, 1992, at Aqueduct, Cordero suffered his last accident in a four horse spill. This time, doctors told him pointedly he would be risking his life if he ever rode again. Reluctantly, Cordero retired. With the considerable assistance of his second wife, former jockey Marjorie Clayton, Cordero became a trainer. Clayton had won 71 races in her short career from 1982 through 1985, including one at Saratoga on a horse named Heartless, August 21, 1983. But like many jockeys before him, Cordero could not succeed in his new profession, partially because of horrible luck—one of his top horses, a stakes winning filly named Rogues Walk, died—and because of his inability to get enough quality horses to maintain a stable in New York.

He made an extremely brief return to riding in 1995, riding one day in Puerto Rico and one day in New York, and finally stopped, returning to training. His final numbers as a trainer, 87 victories, 75 seconds and 72 thirds from 688 starts through 1998, were certainly respectable.

Cordero found a new career as a jockey agent for his Puerto Rican protégé, John Velazquez. Velazquez, a son-in-law of trainer Leo O'Brien, was riding in Puerto Rico when Cordero convinced him to come to the United States in March 1990. Velazquez was injured himself in Cordero's 1992 accident, but recovered. He finished in the Top Ten among New York riders in victories every year from 1993 through 2000 before emerging as New York's leading rider in 2001, 2002 and 2003. Only 32, Velazquez will be a force in New York for as long as he wants.

Cordero's world was changed forever on the evening of

January 22, 2001, when his wife was killed by a hit-and-run driver as she was walking home. Cordero was left with five children, five grandchildren and no game plan on how to continue. But he has.

Velazquez gave Cordero an unexpected thrill at the 2003 Saratoga meeting. Benefiting from the incredible record-breaking meet of trainer Todd Pletcher, Velazquez broke Ycaza's record on the 23rd day of the 36-day meet with his 42nd winner. Cordero was overjoyed that Velazquez, who wound up the meet's leading rider, set the new record without the benefit of extra days that Ycaza hadn't had when Saratoga's season was 24 days long. "I chased that guy for 14 years and never got close," Cordero said in the winner's circle after the soft-spoken Velazquez's record-setting winner. Cordero pointed to Velazquez and said, "I feel like I did it through him."

Velazquez will undoubtedly have his own Hall of Fame career. But there will never be another Cordero. "I wanted to be the best," he said in November 2003. "I wanted to show I could ride anywhere."

At Saratoga, there was no one better.

CHAPTER 6

Dave

Saratoga has always been special to jockey Richard Migliore. It's where he watched Affirmed and Alydar's 1978 Travers when he was 14-years-old. He was 17 when he won his first $100,000 race and broke Steve Cauthen's single-season, apprentice earnings record on separate, early August afternoons at Saratoga Race Course. After winning a race there four years later on BC Sal, Migliore proposed to his wife, Carmela, right in front of the Lyrical Ballad Book Store on Phila Street in downtown Saratoga Springs.

Every fall, Migliore, who finished 16th nationally with more than $9.4 million in earnings in 2003, drives up to Saratoga from his Long Island home to do his Christmas shopping. When he reached Saratoga in early November 2002, he had to make an extra stop.

Migliore had ridden Fourstardave, the most famous New York-bred before Funny Cide, in 25 of his 100 starts, including his final 13. Funny Cide won the 2003 Kentucky Derby and Preakness Stakes, but Fourstardave had won the hearts of racing fans at Saratoga years earlier by winning at least one race there for eight consecutive seasons from 1987 through 1994.

It is almost incomprehensible. Given the current frailty of Thoroughbreds, whose average number of starts per year has plunged from 10.2 in 1970 to 6.8 in 2002, it is a considerable accomplishment for a horse to even race at the same track eight consecutive years. To do so at Saratoga, whose short meet is arguably the toughest in the world, is remarkable. Winning a race at Saratoga for eight straight years is an amazing feat, a tribute not only to Fourstardave, but also to his trainer, Leo O'Brien.

Fourstardave 1993, Richard Migliore up.
(Photo Courtesy of Barbara D. Livingston)

That is why, in Saratoga Springs, the small street next to Siro's, the popular restaurant just outside the gates of Saratoga Race Course, was re-named Fourstardave Way. And why a Saratoga stakes race, the Daryl's Joy, a stakes Fourstardave captured twice in his career, was re-named the Fourstardave. When the New York Turf Writers Association created a Fourstardave Award, of course it was to honor special achievement at Saratoga.

One of Fourstardave's Saratoga achievements was running the fastest mile and a sixteenth in the history of New York Thoroughbred racing at any track on turf or dirt. Fourstardave further distinguished himself by winning graded stakes on both surfaces in open company, not just against New York-breds, and twice setting a stakes record in an open grass stakes at Belmont Park, the Poker.

As he headed up the Northway to Saratoga Springs that early November morning in 2002, Migliore couldn't help but think of Foustardave. A couple weeks earlier, at the age of 17. Fourstardave had come out of retirement to visit Belmont Park to promote Showcase Day, an afternoon of stakes races for New York-breds October 19th. Four days before Showcase Day, Fourstardave was jogging on the training track at Belmont Park, when he suffered a fatal heart attack. He died on the track and then became just the fourth Thoroughbred ever to be buried on the grounds of Saratoga Race Course. Fourstardave, A Phenomenon and Mourjane were buried at Clare Court on the backstretch, adjacent to the seven furlong chute off the main track. The brilliant champion filly Go for Wand was buried in the Saratoga infield.

"It was a couple of weeks after he passed away," Migliore said. "I went up to Saratoga like I do every year to do my Christmas shopping. I went to a florist and bought a bouquet of flowers. I wanted to leave them on his grave, even though there wasn't even a headstone yet. He had always been good to me and my family."

Migliore drove to Clare Court. "I went to put the flowers on his grave, and I could not believe it," Migliore said. "I couldn't believe how many bouquets were already there, and cards and peppermints. This was two weeks after he died. There were Fourstardave T-shirts and hats. It overwhelmed me. I was in awe of how much people felt for him."

Owner Richard Bomze knows. He's always known. Yet even he was surprised at the outpouring of emotion when Fourstardave died, October 15th. "The response was remarkable; it was really remarkable," Bomze said. "People felt as if an old friend died. He wasn't a blue blood. He was just a regular guy who did wonderful things."

One of the e-mails Bomze received, read:

"This past August, I had the pleasure of
meeting you at the NYTHA (New York

Thoroughbred Horsemen's Association,
Bomze is the president) dinner at the
Saratoga Golf Course. I approached you
after the dinner, and you were kind enough
to speak with me about Fourstardave for
several minutes. You allowed me to bend
your ear as I told you how much I truly
loved and admired your horse, and I am
deeply saddened over his passing.

"You see, Mr. Bomze, Saratoga holds a
special place in my heart—so much that my
license plate reads '4TOGA.' I visit the town
quite often, and one of my most treasured
memories was watching your horse win
year after year. For, as steeped in tradition
and history as that town is, if you asked
10,000 people what is the first thing that
comes to their mind when they hear the
word 'Saratoga,' I guarantee that the majority would reply 'Fourstardave.' You can be
certain that Fourstardave will never be forgotten."

Winning a race there for eight consecutive years is why,
but that's just part of the reason. He lost races at Saratoga, too,
but never without a fight. "He gave everything he had," his
trainer, Leo O'Brien said. "He ran 110 percent actually. Every
time he went out, he tried his heart out. He didn't particularly
like the soft ground, but he still ran as hard as he could."

When, asked what first pops into his mind when he
hears Fourstardave's name, Bomze said, "How much joy he
brought to us. He had a spirit about him, a tremendous heart
and will to win. That's probably what killed him. He was so
excited to be back on the track."

Bomze and O'Brien's lives with horses are interwoven.
Bomze, now the president of the New York Thoroughbred
Horsemen's Association and former publisher of American
Turf Monthly, got to know O'Brien when one of Bomze's
friends, Sal Taormina, married Leo O'Brien's sister-in-law.

O'Brien, one of 11 children born in Ireland, had migrated to the United States to continue a successful career as a steeplechase rider, a career ended in a gruesome accident at Monmouth Park when O'Brien's skull was nearly crushed by another rider's horse. "He had a terrible accident," Bomze said. "Leo was 80 percent dead."

O'Brien survived and turned to training. His first client was Bomze. "Leo got a horse named Dumb Donna from Frank Whiteley," Bomze said. "She won a few races for me."

But O'Brien returned to Ireland to help his brother, Michael, who'd also been seriously hurt in a racing accident and was trying to make a career training. "Leo wanted to get back to the U.S., and he said, 'Richie, I'm going to buy a horse for you,'" Bomze said.

And he did in Ireland, a jumper Bomze ultimately named Sports Reporter, the title of a football magazine Bomze also published. When the equine Sports Reporter ventured to the United States to continue his career, Leo O'Brien returned with him and stayed.

Sports Reporter subsequently won 11 races, including the King of Spain International Steeplechase at Ligonier, Spain, in 1983, but then broke a leg in a race. "We tried to save him, but we had to put him down," Bomze said. "We were so broken up. We had a great time with him, but it was very sad."

Three years later, O'Brien saddled his first graded stakes winner, Valley Victory, who took 1986 Coaching Club American Oaks. The horse who would define O'Brien's career was a yearling then. And he would have a baby brother just as talented.

Fourstardave was a handsome chestnut with a long white blaze splitting his face. His dam, Broadway Joan, was one of a handful of broodmares Bomze bought with two other partners. The partners also bought the stallion Compliance. So when Broadway Joan, a daughter of Bold Arian out of Courtneys Doll, by Wakefield Tower, failed to make it as a racehorse, she was bred to Compliance. "Probably the most fortunate thing I did was buying that filly for $2,500," Bomze said. "She was sort of a ratty little thing. She couldn't run. I didn't know what to do with her. I had bought a piece of a stallion named Compliance. I bred the two and out came one of the greatest line of horses in America. I could spend $5, $10 million a year buying horses. You can't buy a horse like Dave. They just come along once every 100 years. That's why we're in the game."

Broadway Joan's first foal, Joan's Dancer, won his first start, but broke his ankle in his second at Aqueduct.

Her second foal made history.

Fourstardave was born April 2, 1985, at Dutch Acres Farm in Hudson, New York. Bomze named Broadway Joan's colt for one of his writers, Dave Piermont. "He was a handicapper and a football writer," Bomze said. "Dave always said he had a four-star play for me every week."

Fourstardave was one of three yearlings Bomze sent to Tony Everard, who ran Another Episode Farm in Ocala, Florida, where O'Brien schooled his young horses. "Tony called me up in January and said, 'Sell two and keep one,'" O'Brien related.

Fourstardave was the keeper, even though he would be gelded before his first start. "He came up to me when he was two in April at Belmont Park," O'Brien said. "When we worked him, we knew right away he could run. Even as a baby."

O'Brien's son, Keith, had just finished his freshman year at Holy Cross, where he studied history and political science. "That summer, I galloped horses for my dad," Keith said. One of them was a handful, a two-year-old named Fourstardave.

"He was tough on me," said Keith, who graduated college, became a steeplechase jockey and now is a trainer, sharing the same New York barn with his dad. "For me, I was young and learning," Keith said. "He was very strong for a two-year-old. He was a handful coming home. From the first time he was in the barn when he was two, he'd make you take notice of him. Some horses force you to take note."

Keith also quickly noted Fourstardave's ability. "We

knew from the beginning he had something special," Keith said.

The timing could not have been better. Leo O'Brien's stable of 10 lacked a headliner, and Keith's education was expensive. "I felt a lot of pressure, self-imposed, not from my dad," Keith said. "There were many mornings I was sweating bullets because we always thought this horse had some ability. We grew up together, in a manner of speaking. If it wasn't for Fourstardave, we wouldn't have been able to afford college. He put me through college and put my Dad on the map. He made it possible for my dad to get better horses. We were indebted to him. He tried harder than any horse I've been around. It was grit, a will to win, a will to please. He'd just give you everything he had. You're heart goes out to him. Such a majestic animal."

Fourstardave would race through his 10-year-old season, making 100 starts under 18 different jockeys at 13 different racetracks. His success at one of them, Saratoga, would become a legend, and he would be dubbed in American Turf Montly by Bomze as the Sultan of Saratoga.

The name fit. Fourstardave's first 11 career starts at Saratoga were in stakes, and he won six of them over the course of five years. "He made everybody's life different," Bomze said. "That's why we're in the game."

Fourstardave won 21 of his 100 starts—though he was zero-for-21 at Aqueduct—with 18 seconds and 16 thirds, and he retired as the all-time leading money winning New York-bred with $1,636,737 in earnings. That total has subsequently been topped three times.

No horse is ever going to top his streak at Saratoga. "It was strange what happened to him when he came to Saratoga," O'Brien said. "He really liked the hot weather. He loved Saratoga and the people loved him back."

O'Brien guesses that he, as well as a lot of people, did not catch on to Fourstardave's fondness for Saratoga the first couple years he won races there. "Until about the fourth year," O'Brien said. "When he won the fourth year, I said, 'Gee, this horse really loves Saratoga.'"

Thought Fourstardave will be remembered as a middle distance grass horse, his one and only start at Saratoga as a two-year-old, August 28, 1987, was in the Empire Stakes for New York-breds at six furlongs on dirt. Fourstardave won by 2 1/2 lengths under Randy Romero. Jose Estrada had ridden Fourstardave in his first two career starts at Belmont Park, a maiden win on June 12th and a second in an allowance race. Bomze remembers Fourstardave's debut: "There was supposed to be a killer horse in there, a real speedball. He couldn't lose, and Dave buried him. He went right by him in the stretch. Then we knew we had something pretty good."

His victory in the Empire Stakes confirmed it. "It was a muddy, muddy day," Bomze said. "When we went to take the picture in the winner's circle, the mud was up to my ankles. I didn't care. It could have been up to my head and I wouldn't have cared. I was so happy."

O'Brien began a pattern of sending Fourstardave to Florida every winter for time off. "We'd send him back to Ocala," O'Brien said. "That was the route we took every year: two months off, two months of training in Florida and then up to me."

As he would throughout Fourstardave's career, O'Brien deflected credit for his success. "It didn't have anything to do with me," he said. "It was the horse. My part was easy. He was super easy to train. The good ones are easy to train."

Even so, Fourstardave was hyper. "He was a real work horse," O'Brien said. "He was real aggressive. He wanted to work fast. He wanted to train fast. He wanted to run fast. You had to slow him down."

O'Brien meant that literally. Fourstardave developed a habit of walking in his stall constantly until O'Brien found a solution. "He was a nervous horses in a sense," O'Brien said. "We cut a hole, like a window, in his stall so he could see his brother (Fourstars Allstar) in the next stall to get him to stop walking. It settled him down."

That was not a problem with Bomze's Fourstars Allstar,

a full brother three years younger than Fourstardave who earned just a tad less, $1,596,750, from 14 wins, 14 seconds and nine thirds in 59 starts.

"They were completely different, like chalk and cheese," O'Brien said. "Fourstars Allstar was laid back. He didn't give a diddly about anything. But he had tremendous heart like Fourstardave."

Fourstars Allstar gave O'Brien and Bomze an unbelievable rush when he shipped to Ireland and won the 1991 Irish 2000 Guineas at The Curragh, becoming the first American-based horse to win a European classic race. "I was very happy with that," O'Brien said. "My mother and father-in-law, all my sisters and brothers, friends, everybody came to see the race. It was televised live in Ireland and England." Afterwards, legendary trainer Vincent O'Brien, who is not related to Leo, stopped by to speak with O'Brien and Bomze. "Vincent O'Brien came over and congratulated us that we had the courage to do it," Leo said.

Those were heady days for O'Brien, but he was too rooted to reality to expect great horses like the Fourstar brothers to happen along every year. "There's a lot of ups and downs in racing," O'Brien said. "You think you'll always have a good horse. But it doesn't happen."

It did at Saratoga for eight years.

When Fourstardave returned to Saratoga as a three-year-old in 1988, he had already won the Grade 2 St. Paul Derby at Canterbury Downs under Daryl Montoya. "It was on dirt, and I think it was one of the best races he ran," O'Brien said.

At Saratoga that summer, Fourstardave won the Albany Stakes for state-breds by a nose under Angel Cordero, Jr. "A lot of different jockeys rode him and he did well for all of them," Cordero said. "He was a sweetheart to ride, and could run all day. He was very talented."

O'Brien had always suspected Fourstardave would be better on grass than he was on dirt, and he decided to test his conviction after the Albany Stakes. Keith O'Brien was up on

Fourstardave on the turf course at the Oklahoma Training Track with instructions from his dad to work him three furlongs. "It was his first time on grass," Keith said. "He went way too fast, three furlongs in :35 or :34 and change. I thought my dad would be annoyed with me, but when I got back to the barn, he was delighted. He was right. My dad always thought he might be better on grass."

Fourstardave made his grass debut under Cordero in the Gallant Man Stakes, finishing fourth, then spent the rest of his three-year-old season finding out just how talented he was on both dirt and grass. On dirt, he finished sixth in the Grade 1 Jerome Handicap at Belmont Park under Robbie Davis and fourth under Herb McCauley in the Pennsylvania Derby at Philadelphia Park.

Returning to grass, Fourstardave finished a close third behind Steinlen and Mac's Fighter in the $200,000 Laurel Dash, October 21, 1988, with Cordero riding. The O'Briens thought he had won the race. "There were two finish lines at Laurel because they had the Laurel International (a major grass stakes attracting international competition) going on," Keith said. "He was about 30-1. Angel rode him to the first wire. Me and my Dad were jumping up and down. We thought he won. Then we realized, 'Oh-oh.'" Fourstardave raced to the next finish line and finished third but was only beaten a half length and a nose by Steinlen, who would run second in the Breeders' Cup Mile to the brilliant filly Miesque in his very next start. The following year, Steinlen would win the Breeders' Cup Mile and be named 1989 Grass Champion, only making Fourstardave's performance against him even better. Keith hardly needed the validation. "That race got me through the whole winter at school," he said.

When Keith returned to school, Dave was galloped by his dad, then for the rest of his career by Joe Hennessy, a former steeplechase rider in Ireland who is now a trainer.

Dave finished his three-year-old season by running 10th on grass in the Grade 1 Hollywood Derby with Chris McCarron aboard, then third in two dirt starts at Aqueduct, the Joe Palmer Stakes and a handicap race.

Though he'd only won two of 13 starts at three, he had also finished second once and third six times, posting his highest earnings year, $377,139, a testimony to the company he was facing.

And he already had a Saratoga following. Faye Kling, a social service worker for Montgomery County, New York, dragged her husband, Nick, a farmer, to breakfast at Saratoga Race Course one August afternoon in 1988. Neither had ever been to the track. While she was there, Faye walked around the grounds, got lost and happened to meet an exercise rider atop a horse. She reached out her hand to pet the horse. The horse snorted. "And it went all over my shirt," she said. "It didn't bother me. I used to ride horses. I saw Fourstardave's name on the saddle pad." Faye not only became an instant Fourstardave fan—to the point where she would hang out at Leo O'Brien's barn in the mornings and walk Fourstardave— but helped convince her husband to change careers. He became a handicapper and racing writer for the *Amsterdam Recorder* in 1992, and moved on to the *Troy Record*, his present employer, in 1998, while also serving as co-host to the weekly OTB-cable TV show "Track Facts" with Tom Amello, a high school teacher in his normal life.

At the age of four, Fourstardave made three Saratoga starts. After finishing second by half a length to Highland Springs in the Daryl's Joy, Fourstardave took on Steinlen again in the Bernard Baruch Handicap with Migliore riding for the first time. Fourstardave finished fourth by 7 3/4 lengths as Steinlen jogged at 2-5 on the way to being named Champion Grass Horse that year. Undeterred, Fourstardave bounced back to win the West Point Handicap for New York-breds by one length, also on grass, 10 days later, keeping his Saratoga streak intact.

"He was as honest as any horse I've ever ridden," Migliore said. "I can't put any horse above him on that. And he had a great deal of charisma. He liked the attention."

Truth be known, he was getting plenty of attention from O'Brien, who was well aware of the backstretch adage that one should never get emotionally attached to his horse. "Everybody does," O'Brien said. "It's because of the love of the horse. You really get attached to them. They're like your kids.

"He was a very smart horse. He was extremely intelligent as horses go. He was a real ham. He loved people, and he responded very much to me, to my voice. I would go back every evening, and when he heard my voice, he'd run to the front of the stall and start whinnying. I'd go up to him, pick up some grass, or give him a little more feed. O'Brien discovered Dave liked bee pollen, used as a vitamin supplement for horses, and gave it to him as a treat.

He'd earned it.

At the age of five, Fourstardave won four of 14 starts. At Saratoga, he won the Daryl's Joy by 2 1/2 lengths and finished second in the West Point under Mike Smith, who rode Fourstardave in 31 of his 100 starts.

But Fourstardave would begin to reach his peak the following summer at the age of six. First, he won the 1991 Daryl's Joy by three lengths, covering the mile and sixteenth in 1:38 4/5 (1:38.91), faster than any horse had ever run the distance on turf or dirt at any track in New York racing history. He did so ridden out—his jockey, Smith; never lifted his whip. That mark remains the Saratoga Main Turf Course record and still compares favorably with the existing world records for that distance on turf—1:38 by Told—and on dirt—Hopedown's Day's 1:38 2/5.

"Every year when he went to Saratoga, it was amazing to watch him," Keith O'Brien said. "He always turned it up a notch. He was almost human. He knew what Saratoga meant to my family. My dad's been coming to Saratoga since 1964. Dave knew where he was and he knew, 'I had to raise my game here.'"

Fourstardave won his second 1991 Saratoga start, the West Point, by four lengths exactly three weeks later.

When he returned to Saratoga in 1992 as a seven-year-old, his Saratoga streak was on most people's minds. Most, not all. "Trainers can't think of streaks," O'Brien said. "You just want him to run good every year."

Fourstardave failed to do that in his first two starts that summer, finishing a distant fifth in the Daryl's Joy when it came off the turf and fourth by three lengths to Wild Cataract in the West Point.

On August 24, 1992, Fourstardave did something he had never done at Saratoga: compete in an allowance race. All his previous starts there had been in stakes. With his streak at stake, Fourstardave won that allowance race by two lengths, extending his streak to six—six straight seasons of winning a race at Saratoga.

Any thoughts of Dave slowing down at the age of eight in 1993 were put to rest by his performance in the Grade 3 Poker Stakes at Belmont. Re-united with Migliore, who had ridden Dave five times earlier, four times in 1989 and once in 1991, Dave broke his own stakes record, winning by 2 1/4 lengths in 1:33 1/5 for the mile, his last start before heading north to Saratoga for three races. Migliore would ride Dave in his last 13 starts and 19 of his final 20, the lone absence when Dave journeyed to Hong Kong at the end of 1993.

In his first 1993 start at Saratoga, Dave finished a solid second to grass star Lure in the Daryl's Joy. Then he won a handicap on grass by 2 1/2 lengths, extending his Saratoga streak to seven years.

His third start that summer was spectacular and incredibly disheartening for his connections. It was also one of the bravest performances by any Thoroughbred in Saratoga's long history.

In the 1993 West Point Handicap, August 26th, Fourstardave, carrying 125 pounds including Migliore, stumbled severely at the break. His head came within a foot of hitting the ground, but Migliore somehow kept him upright, and Dave regained his balance. He was last in the field of seven.

"It was one of the most impressive performances I was ever involved with," Migliore said. "He nearly fell down. It's amazing he even got off the ground. He was carrying a lot of weight."

The poor start meant Fourstardave would have to

change running styles. "He was a horse who always had a high cruising speed, and he liked to be near the front," Migliore said. "But he had to come from behind that day."

And he did. Under patient handling by Migliore, who did not panic, Dave moved up into fourth heading into the first turn. He made his move in the upper stretch, and was surrounded by horses on his inside and outside, But he had gained a short lead and refused to yield, holding off Excellent Tipper, who was carrying five pounds less, by a neck.

"And the beat goes on," announcer Tom Durkin said. "The old boy has done it again."

But there was a claim of foul by Dennis Carr, whose horse had finished fourth. "He minimally brushed the horse making a little room at the three-sixteenths pole," Migliore said. "He had won and was placed fifth. It was a travesty that day. Nobody deserved to win a race more."

He gets no argument from Bomze. "I was numb," Bomze said. "I was just so numb. I just couldn't move because it was probably one of the most thrilling runs I've ever seen."

Durkin said afterwards, "He was just going to finish first and that was going to be it. There was nothing that was going to stop him, no act of God, nature or a starting gate, for that matter, that was going to stop him from winning."

Regardless, Fourstardave was disqualified. He ended his eight-year-old season in Hong Kong, finishing 12th in the $4 million Hong Kong International Bowl.

Fourstardave came to Saratoga winless in his first five starts at the age of nine. He was fourth in an allowance race and second by 2 3/4 lengths in the Kingston Handicap for state-breds at Belmont Park, then third in the Grade 3 Red Bank Handicap at Monmouth. Returning to Belmont Park, Dave was fifth to Nijinsky's Gold in the Jaipur Stakes and nosed by Dominant Prospect in the Poker, both Grade 3 stakes.

Dave was entered in an allowance race, July 24, 1994, attempting to extend his Saratoga streak to eight years, and it would be televised by CBS (CBS was covering the Go for Wand

Handicap later that afternoon). Hank Goldberg told his CBS audience that "Fourstardave is a wonderful story. You'd love to see him win. He's a commoner in a world of royalty."

He had drawn the rail in the field of seven going one mile, making his 93rd career start.

Migliore let Dave settle in third on the backstretch, maybe six lengths behind two dueling leaders. And then Dave went after them.

His progress was immediate. Durkin announced, "Fourstardave is poised in third position. He's only a length and a half from the lead."

Then he got closer. "And now Migliore makes his move with the old boy," Durkin called. "There goes Fourstardave and he sweeps to a short lead as the field turns for home."

The crowd let out such a roar that the building seemed to shake.

Dave came out of the far turn a bit wide, but it didn't matter. He started to draw away. "Fourstardave is one furlong away from eight years worth of Saratoga victories," Durkin cried. "The legend lives on! Fourstardave wins again at the Spa!"

A year later, Durkin described that moment: "I'll never forget the roar that that crowd gave last year when Fourstardave made that move on the turn. I mean, goose pimple time. The roof of that 125-year-old track just came charging up. It was a wonderful, wonderful thrill, maybe the thrill of my race-calling life."

This from the man who remains the only announcer in the Breeders' Cup's 20-year history.

Fourstardave's reward was the most difficult assignment of his career.

Fourstardave was asked to take on not one grass superstar in the 1994 Bernard Baruch Handicap, but two: Lure and Paradise Creek. Going into that race, Lure's grass record was 10 wins and five seconds in 15 starts. Paradise Creek had won six straight races, beating Lure in two of them. Yet in the Bernard Baruch field of five, Fourstardave went off at 9-2, and

he led his four rivals for much of the mile and an eighth before
he took a bad step. "The race he got hurt was one of his best
races," O'Brien said. "He was three lengths in front of Lure and
Paradise Creek. He stepped in a hole and broke a cannon bone
in his right front. It was a shock. He never had a pimple on
him."

Richard Migliore
(*Photo Courtesy of Barbara D. Livingston*)

Incredibly, Fourstardave still finished third, seven lengths behind Lure, who beat Paradise Creek by a length. "He was never the same the next year," Bomze said. "He just wasn't the same horse."

At the age of 10, Fourstardave finished seventh vs. New York-breds in the 1995 Kingston Stakes, then fourth in the Grade 3 Jaipur Handicap. He lost an allowance race at Belmont, then at Saratoga finished fifth, fourth, and in his final start, August 27th, fifth in allowance company.

"So we stopped racing him," Bomze said. "That was very hard because when you go to the racetrack and everybody knows your horse, you're on top of the world."

His final record at Saratoga was eight wins, six of them in stakes, three seconds, two thirds, four fourths and four fifths in 21 starts. And a lifetime of memories.

Fourstardave was retired and placed in Tony Everard's care at Another Episode Farm in Ocala. "Tony would gallop him all the time," Bomze said. "That's where Dave lived. He was running. He was happy. He had his own paddock. He had a marvelous life. He had a better life than 99 percent of all people have. Tony took great care of him."

So did O'Brien, who said he couldn't even look at a horse after he saw Fourstardave's fatal heart attack at Belmont Park on that sad October morning in 2002. Keith O'Brien had galloped him the day before. "He was going to be paraded in the Showcase," Keith said. "We thought, 'Let's give him a little gallop.' I got nostalgic. I was remembering way back when I gave him a gallop and I remember thinking even while he's 17, he feels better than all the horses we had now. If you could bottle what he had, I'd be a rich man."

The next morning, exercise rider Damien Rock got on Dave for a light gallop. "He was dead when he hit the ground," said Keith, who was galloping another horse at the time. "I came back from the track and my dad said, 'Fourstardave just died.' I said, 'Oh, my God.' It was sad and gut wrenching, but it was almost like he came home to die, in a poetic sense. He started off at Belmont and I got on him one more time before he died. To me, he came back to give me one more thrill."

There were so many.

"I have all his races, so I can watch them," Leo O'Brien said. "When I feel down, I put a race on, have a cup of tea, watch him win and feel real good. I had so much pride in the horse. You had a big warm feeling in your chest."

Migliore knows that feeling. "It was great just to be associated with him," he said. "Walking around at Saratoga, you weren't just a jockey. You were Fourstardave's jockey."

CHAPTER 7

Oops!

She was a perfectly innocent three-year-old filly doing an honest day's work. Allumeuse's future seemed bright as she walked into the starting gate at Saratoga Race Course, August 2, 1986, a mile and a sixteenth allowance race on the main turf course. Later that day, the outstanding filly, Lady's Secret, would challenge males in the $250,000 Grade 1 Whitney Handicap.

Allumeuse's assignment was less daunting. She would face nine other fillies looking for their second career victory. Owned by Eric N. Kronfeld, an art attorney in the music business, the bay daughter of Robellino out of For the Flag, by Forli, was trained by Tom Skiffington, Jr., a former steeplechase rider who led the country in earnings three times, in 1976, 1978 and 1979.

Allumeuse was unraced at two, then floundered in her first three starts at three, finishing 11th, seventh and fifth in three maiden dirt races at Gulfstream Park and Hialeah. But Kronfeld and Skiffington knew Allumeuse would do better on grass. And she did. She never raced on dirt again.

Skiffington is the son of an Air Force B-52 pilot, Col. Tom Skiffington, who served in Vietnam for four years and was a base commander in Seoul, Korea. Skiffington's mom rode jumpers and show horses, and Skiffington got an opportunity to follow her passion when his dad was assigned to the Pentagon and the family moved to Middleburg, Virginia, when he was 15.

After riding in jump races in the U.S. and Europe, Skiffington changed careers. He worked for several outstanding trainers, including Burley Cocks, Frank Whiteley and Phil Johnson, all in the Hall of Fame, before opening his own stable. All helped him with his career, as did yet another Hall of Fame trainer, Woody Stephens.

Marshall Jenney (head of Derry Meeting Farm in Unionville, Pennsylvania), who bred Stephens' outstanding racehorse and prolific sire Danzig, also bred Mrs. Penny, a champion filly at the age of two and three in England. As a four-year-old in 1980, she won two of three starts, both Group 1 stakes, in France, and finished second twice and third twice in four starts in England and Ireland. Kornfeld decided to ship her home to the United States, in 1981. Jenney knew Skiffington from his steeplechase days and recommended him to Kronfeld, who sent the mare to him. At the time, Skiffington was training just six horses. "He wanted the filly to run long on the grass and somebody who knew European training," Skiffington said. "It was certainly a huge break for me to get a filly of that quality. It was a big help in my career. I did well with Mrs. Penny (she won the Grade 3 Queen Charlotte Handicap at The Meadowlands and finished second against colts in the Grade 2 Manhattan Handicap at Belmont Park), and it snowballed from there. He kept sending me horses. And that's how I got Allumeuse. He bred her. She was bred to run long on grass. I got her late in her two-year-old year. I liked her. I thought she was going to be a good mile-and-a-quarter or mile-and-a-half grass horse. She had a real good turn of foot. I didn't know whether she was going to go on to be the best in her division, but she had a chance to be."

Allumeuse made her first grass start on April 2, 1986, at Hialeah, and finished an improved second in a mile-and-a-six-teenth maiden race. Skiffington shipped north to Belmont

Park and Allumeuse finished third in another mile-and-a-six-teenth maiden race on grass. When Skiffington stretched her out to a mile-and-a-quarter, she won by a length and three-quarters, June 23rd.

In her first start in allowance company, she finished fifth in a field of 11 at a mile-and-a-quarter, July 5th at Belmont. Skiffington pointed her to Saratoga.

"Saratoga has been one of those places for me where I've had the best days of my life and the worst days of my life," Skiffington said. "When I was 19, I rode in my first race at Saratoga, a steeplechase, and I won on Madagascar for Sidney Watters. He won and paid over a hundred dollars. Three days later, I fell looking for my whip. A horse ran over me. I was out six weeks with a broken shoulder, a broken collarbone and a fractured skull."

On opening day of the 1986 Saratoga meet, Skiffington's Mourjane won the Daryl's Joy Stakes. Allumeuse made her Saratoga debut the next day, August 2, 1986, with Jose Santos aboard from the seven post. She was No. 8 on the program, but the four horse, Image Of Class, scratched, allow-ing her to move inside one stall. Bettors thought she had a realistic chance in a wide-open race and sent her off at odds of 7.20-to-1, the exact same odds as the No. 11 filly breaking from the far outside, Syntonic, ridden by apprentice Wigberto Paneto.

Three horses vied for favortism. The tepid betting choice at 3.20-to-1 was Legacy Of Strength, one of three four-year-old fillies in the race, ridden by Pat Day. Another four-year-old, Chehana, was 3.40-to-1 under Angel Cordero, Jr. Edgewater, ridden by Jorge Velasquez, would go off at 3.90-to-1 (7-2). The other four-year-old in the field, Roberto's Social, was sent off at 8.20-to-1 under Randy Romero.

All the other fillies went off at double-digit odds. Dawn's Fancy was 12-1; Utah Pine, the No. 6 horse, 16-1; and Festivity, the No. 2 horse ridden by Jean Cruguet, 25-1. The longest price in the race was the No. 3 horse, Fasta Dancer, rid-den by Jerry Bailey at 33-1.

The main players in what turned out to be the most infamous race in Saratoga history were:

No. 1 ➤ Dawn's Fancy
     2 ➤ Festivity
     3 ➤ Fasta Dancer
     6 ➤ Utah Pine
     8 ➤ Allumeuse
   11 ➤ Syntonic

John Pricci was one of the handicappers/columnists covering the Saratoga meet for Newsday on Long Island. He also happened to be the president of the New York Turf Writer's Association. He liked Allumeuse enough to make her his best bet of the day. He also bet $50 to win on her. That would be a return of $410.00 if she finished first.

Dave Zyglewicz liked Allumeuse, too. Ziggy was a local boxing legend who was 32-4 with 18 knockouts. On April 22, 1969, Ziggy fought Joe Frazier for the heavyweight championship of the world in Houston, Texas. Smokin Joe scored a technical knockout (TKO) in the first round. Ziggy returned to Watervliet, just north of Albany, where he ran a successful tavern called Ziggy's Corner.

Because Allumeuse was in the second race, Zyglewicz bet her in Daily Double tickets. He had a $24 live Daily Double ticket after Cordero won the first race on Passing Thunder at 9-2. The $2 Daily Double of Passing Thunder and Allumeuse was paying $97, so he stood to get back $1,164 if she won.

She won, but Ziggy, like John Pricci, is still waiting to be paid 18 years later.

There are three stewards and a handful of patrol and placing judges at New York's racetracks entrusted with enforcing the rules of racing. They come into play whenever they see a foul—such as a horse interfering with another horse's path—or when a jockey or trainer raises an objection claiming his horse has been fouled during the running of a race. Usually, the allegation concerns interference.

At Saratoga Race Course, the three stewards represent three different entities: the New York Racing Association, the Jockey Club and the State Racing and Wagering Board. On August 2, 1986, the Jockey Club steward was Dick McLaughlin and the State Racing and Wagering Board steward was Sal Ferrara. Jerry Burke was the NYRA steward, but he was tending to his ill wife and missed all of the Saratoga meet. An alternate steward, Robert F. "Tony" Kelley, Jr., was Burke's replacement that afternoon at Saratoga.

Dick Hamilton, now the Communications Officer with the National Museum of Racing and Hall of Fame, was one of three patrol judges that day, stationed in the patrol tower at the half-mile pole on the backstretch, half a mile from the finish line. Two other patrol judges were strategically placed at the quarter pole and at the finish line.

This race unfolded with Bailey gunning his longshot, Fasta Dancer, to the lead from the three post, while the apprentice rider Paneto hustled up his horse, Syntonic, to contest the pace on Fasta Dancer's outside. They were first and second from the beginning of the race until the head of the stretch. Fasta Dancer led by a length and a half after a quarter of a mile, then by just a head after half a mile and also after three-quarters of a mile until Syntonic began to inch away in the stretch.

"I can remember like it was yesterday," Bailey said in November, 2003. "The horse with the shadow roll (Syntonic) was second to me the whole way, right on my flank. Then, she was half a length in front of me."

That is when Syntonic knocked Fasta Dancer right into the hedge on the inside of the grass course. Fasta Dancer and Bailey went down.

"I remember, as I was falling, I said, 'God protect me,'" Bailey said. "I fell like I was on a pillow. I landed as soft as you can possibly land. I was never sore. I wasn't sore the next day."

Robbie Davis, riding Utah Pine, who had been behind Fasta Dancer, wasn't as fortunate. Utah Pine fell over Fasta Dancer, hurtling Davis to the ground. "I was in behind all the action," Davis said. "My horse fell behind Jerry's. I was laid out pretty good on the track. I came to find out I wasn't injured, but I was shaken up pretty good. I took a pretty good jolt."

Both jockeys and both fallen horses escaped serious injury.

Syntonic, meanwhile, was trying to hold on to her lead. She couldn't. Out in the middle of the track, Santos had Allumeuse rolling, and she crossed the wire a length and a half in front of 25-1 longshot Festivity, who beat the tiring Syntonic by two lengths for second. Dawn's Fancy was fourth, another two lengths behind Syntonic.

On the toteboard, the numbers of the first four finishers were posted: 8, 2, 11 and 1. And, of course, the inquiry sign lit up immediately, standard procedure following any incident when one horse, let alone two, go down.

Then all hell broke loose.

Bailey got up, walked from the sixteenth pole to the finish line, crossed the dirt course and headed for the winner's circle, where a phone is set up so stewards can speak directly to the jockeys. Bailey said he remembers his phone conversation with the steward verbatim:

"The steward said, 'Can you enlighten us on what happened out there?'" Bailey said. "I said, 'Yeah, the horse that was tracking me the whole way got in front of me mid-stretch and pushed me right into the hedge.' They said, 'Thank you.'"

Bailey walked back to the jockey's room.

When a horse is involved in a possible foul, his number on the tote board begins flashing. But instead of the 11, the number flashing on the board was the 8, Allumeuse.

The only way that would make sense was if Allumeuse was involved in an incident other than the one in mid-stretch, when Paneto's horse clearly pushed Bailey's horse into the hedge in front of thousands of witnesses with Allumeuse nowhere near the scene of the crime.

Stewards investigating a race always talk to the jockey of the horse who allegedly committed the foul. That meant a phone conversation with Santos after the initial conversation with Bailey.

Santos has been one of the top jockeys in the world for the last 20 years. His English has improved somewhat in the past two decades, but it is still sometimes difficult to understand him, especially on the phone. That was evident in the Miami Herald's completely false story that Santos had used a buzzer to win the 2003 Kentucky Derby on Funny Cide. The reporter who interviewed Santos by phone thought Santos had said, "Q ring," as part of an answer to a question when Santos had said "curing."

So speaking to Santos on the phone 17 years earlier was an adventure, but he had been riding in Florida and New York for two years and his English was beginning to improve.

Here is how Santos remembers it:

"The clerk of scales said the stewards wanted to talk to me. I said, 'Sure.' I grab the phone and they say, 'You know what happened?' I said, 'I know what happened. Two guys went down on the inside rail.' They say, 'You caused the problem.' I said, 'What?' They said, 'You caused the problem on the inside.' I said, 'I think you're picking the wrong horse.' He said, 'No, I'm pretty sure it was your fault.' I said, 'Sir, I think you're making a mistake.' I said it twice. The steward said, 'We are going to look at the tape.'"

Migliore had overheard part of the discussion: "Jose didn't speak English as well as he does now, but I remember him saying, 'You've got the wrong horse.' I distinctly remember that."

Skiffington watched the race from a clubhouse box seat. Kronfeld was not there, which may have been a blessing. "It was a rather bizarre thing," Skiffington said in December 2003. "She won and then the lights started flashing. I remember she came down the center of the course and won pretty easily. I thought something had happened on the turn or at the start. So I'm there sitting, waiting for the replay to come on."

It never did.

Skiffington walked down to the winner's circle to speak with Santos. "I was using Santos a lot in Florida earlier that year," Skiffington said. "He was winning everything, and I started using him. I jumped on his bandwagon early."

Skiffington asked Santos what was going on. Santos replied, 'They're blaming me." Skiffington said, "They're crazy. They're making a mistake."

Not as big as their next one.

In an instant of insanity, the stewards disqualified Allumeuse; placed her last in the field of 10; changed the order of finish to 2-11-1-9, and made the race official. Once the result is made official, that's it. Announcer Marshall Cassidy told fans that Allumeuse was disqualified for interference.

When a horse is disqualified, a head-on shot of the incident is shown on all the TV monitors at the track. The offending horse is highlighted in a box so he is easily followed, and an announcer walks fans through the incident to explain the disqualification. But the only people who saw this head-on shot were reporters in the press box. The 43,520 fans at Saratoga Race Course as well as bettors at off-track parlors throughout the state and at Aqueduct for simulcasting were left on their own to figure out what had transpired.

In the jockey's room, everyone was stunned. "I could not believe it," Bailey said. "I said, 'How could they take that horse down? Maybe it was the fact that the winner had a shadow roll (a wide strap placed across a horse's nose to keep the horse from seeing shadows on the ground) and so did Paneto's horse. That was the only thing I could possibly think of. What amazed me is that three people of high intelligence all made the same mistake. They weren't dummies. It was pretty amazing."

Santos called the stewards from the jockey's room and said, "Sir, you made a mistake."

Pricci, who thought the stewards had been looking at the second or the third place finisher, raced to the steward's booth just around the corner from the press box.

"When they took down the winner, I bolted out of

there," Pricci said. "I was enraged. I knew that she wasn't the horse in question. As far as I could tell, Allumeuse was in the middle of the track."

When Pricci reached the steward's booth, he asked, "Gentlemen, can I speak to you?"

They said he could.

Pricci asked, "Gentlemen, can you tell me what the thinking was on the disqualification?"

One of the stewards told Pricci it was for interfering with another horse that caused the accident.

Pricci said, "Gentlemen, I respectfully submit that you took down the wrong horse."

Pricci knew he was right: "I knew they had the wrong license plate. I knew they had the wrong horse."

Then he showed them.

Pricci asked them to show the replay on the monitor in the stewards room. "I pointed to the monitor," Pricci said. "And the monitor was showing a head-on of the stretch or a three-quarter pan coming from the front. It was definitely a forward view."

Pricci asked what Allumeuse had done to warrant the disqualification.

One of the stewards told Pricci what he thought had happened.

Pricci replied, "That's wrong."

Pricci literally put his finger on the monitor to identify horses, and said, "This is Syntonic. This is Allumeuse. You can see Syntonic bearing in. The other horse didn't do any-thing."

That's all he needed to say. "They were stunned, and I didn't wait," Pricci said. "I stormed out like I stormed in. I was hot. I ran out of the stewards stand and back into the press-box. I told everybody, 'They took down the wrong fucking horse!'"

Bettors who had wagered on Festivity, Syntonic and Dawn's Fancy lived out a fantasy without, initially, realizing it. Festivity paid $52 to win and the Daily Double of Passing Shot and Festivity paid $254.40. The quiniela of Festivity and Syntonic paid $285.20. Bettors also cashed in on place and show bets on Festivity, place and show wagers on Syntonic and show bets on Dawn's Fancy.

The flip side, of course, was that a lot of bettors got screwed.

From his position as a patrol judge half a mile from the finish line, Dick Hamilton had seen very little of the second race. "I didn't know anything had happened," he said. "I didn't see the incident. Then, when the patrol car picked me up to go back to the finish line, there was obviously some activity. A horse had fallen into the hedge. I saw that there was an inquiry up. I went on to the next race."

Then paddock and patrol judge, Lucas Dupps, who had been stationed at the finish line, asked Hamilton to work in the paddock for the third race. "He asked me to put the riders up for the next race, because he said, 'There's something I had to check,'" Hamilton said.

Hamilton obliged, calling "riders up" and the jockeys in the third race mounted their horses and began walking them from the paddock onto the track. "One of the first horses to go by me was Angel Cordero, Jr.'s (Lucky Touch)," Hamilton said. "He was on his horse going to the track and he asked me, 'Where were you in the last race?' I said, 'The half-mile pole.' He said, 'They took down the wrong horse.'"

That's a line stewards hear from disgruntled jockeys and trainers every time they disqualify any horse. Hamilton replied, "Well, Angel, that's a matter of opinion."

Cordero said, "No, they took down the wrong horse."

Hamilton said, "Then, it hit me. Lucas had wanted to check something. He said he wanted to check his film (of the incident) and check his notes (from the race). Then it dawns on me that he had to report the incident to the stewards. I said, 'Maybe there is something.' I didn't need to know. I had nothing to do with the reporting. The last thing they needed was someone else asking questions."

There were so many, none more germane than the one

Bailey asked: "How could three intelligent people make the same mistake?"

Reporters waited for hours for a statement from NYRA and/or the stewards and were not allowed into the steward's booth. Finally, after the last race, the stewards came to the press box and admitted their mistake.

The New York State Racing and Wagering Board investigated. The Albany *Times Union* did its own investigation, producing an excellent article by Tim Layden, who is now with *Sports Illustrated*, which ran one year and one week after the race. Layden explored four factors. The first three had already been made public:

1) There were five stewards in the stewards' booth when the second race went off. Alternate stewards Charlie Sullivan, who was also the clerk of scales, and John Russo were in the booth as well as Kelley, McLaughlin and Ferrara.

2) The phone call from the patrol judge who did see the incident, Lucas Dupps, to the stewards booth—which is standard procedure—was never related to the three stewards who made the disqualification. Dupps told Layden, "I put my binoculars down and said, 'Lucas calling stewards,' just like I always do," Dupps told Layden. "The voice on the other end said, 'Come in, Lucas.' I said, 'Coming into the stretch, the 11 horse (Syntonic) crowded the 3 horse (Fasta Dancer), causing him to lose his balance and fall.'"

According to Layden's story, Sullivan took that call from Dupps. Sullivan maintains he relayed Dupps' message. Layden wrote. "The stewards unanimously agree that they never heard (from) him," and that McLaughlin woke up in the middle of the night and asked himself, "What happened to Lucas' phone call? I couldn't wait to get to the track the next day and ask him what happened."

(To this day, Dupps, now 85 and retired, wonders the same thing. "When you get a call from the patrol judge, you always relay it to the other stewards," Dupps said in January 2004. "Why whomever took my call never relayed the message, I have no idea. How they overlooked that, I don't know.")

3) According to Layden's story, McLaughlin alleges Kelley watched a replay of the race, and, when Ferrara and McLaughlin started to watch the replay again, Kelley told them it wasn't necessary to watch again. According to Layden, Kelley admitted saying "It was the winner," to the other stewards, but when he said it, and the details after he said it, were disputed. So was whether or not McLaughlin and Ferrara had seen the head-on replay themselves or had relied on Kelley's word.

Layden presented a fourth factor: the physical layout of the stewards' booth at Saratoga. Stewards were unable to watch the replay and listen to jockeys at the same time because the phones and televisions were in separate rooms, and the booth, glassed in on four sides and adjacent to the announcer's booth, is a "highly disruptive location."

Left unanswered to this day is how anyone who watched the race could not have realized that Syntonic pushed Fasta Dancer into the hedge. They had been running 1-2 next to each other the entire way, and one of them pushed the other into the hedge. You didn't need Columbo for this one.

Worse yet is this question: Since both Bailey and Santos told whomever they were speaking to in the stewards' booth that Allumeuse had nothing to do with the incident, how did Allumeuse get blamed in the first place? The only item common to Allumeuse and Syntonic was that they had shadow rolls and that, in the process of winning the race, Allumeuse had gone past Syntonic in the stretch.

And that was it.

As soon as Pricci walked the stewards through their mistake on the monitor in the stewards' booth, they realized the mistake and the enormous consequences. They never showed the replay on track monitors for fear of "causing a riot," Ferrara said afterwards.

Part of the mistake could be corrected, and was. Syntonic would be disqualified and placed last. Paneto would be suspended for his careless ride. And the purse money would be re-distributed according to the correct order of finish: Allumeuse, Festivity and Dawn's Fancy finishing first, second and third, respectively.

"I won the race for 10 minutes," Festivity's jockey, Jean Cruguet, said. "After that, I lose the race."

Nobody, of course, told the public.

"I waited for the replay, and they never showed it," Skiffington said. "Eight or nine people told me they took down the wrong horse."

Skiffington, who had a horse to saddle in the fourth race, Riposto, with Jean-Luc Samyn riding, called the stewards from the Racing Secretary's office. "They said, 'Come up after you run your horse in the fourth,'" Skiffington said. "They said they'll me show me the replay and show me the disqualification. I figured there had been a malfunction in the camera regarding the replay."

But in the paddock before the fourth race, Santos, riding Slew City Slew, approached Skiffington "He told me that they had disqualified the wrong horse and that by the end of the day, they'd put her (Allumeuse) back as the winner."

Skiffington called the stewards again. "They told me

they had made a dreadful mistake," Skiffington said. "That they had disqualified the wrong horse, and that, after the races, they would put her back as the winner."

When asked of his reaction 17 years later, Skiffington said, "Naturally, I was glad my horse won the race. I didn't feel sorry for the fans because I thought they would make some sort of restitution for the people. It wasn't in my mind that they would go down the tubes. I will tell you one thing. I will tell you this. We're all human and we all make mistakes. The stewards, on the whole, in New York are among the best. I felt bad for those guys. One mistake led to another mistake led to another."

They would pay for those mistakes.

Eleven days after the race, the New York State Racing and Wagering Board demoted Ferrara to Finger Lakes, and he retired.

Kelley was demoted to assistant steward and fined by NYRA. "Oh, God, yes, I deserved it," Kelley told Layden. "I'm lucky that's all I got. I was fined a pretty good amount of money, but I could have lost my job." Kelley continued to work at Saratoga, Belmont Park and Aqueduct until his retirement the next year.

McLaughlin was fined with the stipulation that the money would be contributed to the school of racing officials at the University of Arizona's racetrack industry program. Two weeks later, Ogden Mills "Dinny" Phipps, Chairman of the Jockey Club, asked McLaughlin to accept a desk job in New York City. McLaughlin preferred not to, resigned his post at Belmont Park September 24th and accepted an offer to be a steward at Rockingham Park in New Hampshire, where he had walked hots 40 years ago.

McLaughlin told Layden point blank, "There is no excuse for what happened."

Or for what happened afterwards.

There were a lot of avenues the New York Racing Association and the state of New York could have explored to address the unjust consequences of the wrong horse being disqualified. Of course, redress could only have been made to those bettors on Allumeuse who did not throw away their tickets when she was disqualified. It's reasonable to assume that most of Allumeuse bettors did discard winning tickets upon the announcement of her disqualification and seeing her number come off the tote board.

Of course, an immediate announcement that there had been a mistake would have given Allumeuse bettors a better chance at justice, but that did not happen.

They could have refunded any bets using Allumeuse, and chose not to do so.

They could have paid off the correct winning tickets and they could have funded it painlessly by using a small percentage of the tens of thousands of dollars of uncashed tickets the state gets back every year and uses for its general fund. Uh-uh.

Ziggy didn't throw away his tickets. Instead, he became the first person in the Capital District to file a lawsuit against the parties responsible for turning his $1,164 of winning tickets into zero. At the time, he said, "Ziggy ain't ever gonna give up to the day I die. It's not over."

Ziggy and nine other angry bettors filed suit against the New York Racing Association in small claims court in Saratoga a few days after the race. Filing it in small claims court saved Ziggy the cost of an attorney. NYRA, however, was well represented. "When you sue the state, they send an army against you," Ziggy said. "Three lawyers in small claims court. And their own stenographer. It was real unusual."

Judge Aaron Brenner ruled on December 3 in favor of NYRA. "But he made a footnote in the written decision that legislative action should be taken in this case so it would never happen again," Ziggy said. Brenner said, "There should be some funds set up for mistakes such as this one. It may occur again."

Another suit filed by 11 bettors in the state Supreme Court in Albany had a different outcome: Judge Joseph Torraca ruled November 14th in favor of the bettors, but the case was appealed, and the bettors lost.

The New York State Senate passed a bill, 57-0, April 2, 1987, that would pay off the race's rightful winners from uncashed tickets. That bill, however, died in the State Assembly Ways and Means Committee.

Four other suits also failed.

Sixteen days after the most infamous race in Saratoga history, Allumeuse made her stakes debut at Saratoga, in the $75,000 added Grade 3 Nijana Stakes at a mile and a sixteenth. She finished 10th in a field of 11. "She ran really bad, and we couldn't figure out why," Skiffington said. "We were scratching our heads. Right after the race, she just completely gave up eating."

Skiffington sent the filly to Derry Meeting Farm in Pennsylvania. "They couldn't get her to eat either," he said.

Allumeuse was sent to the New Boulton Veterinary Center. "They took blood tests right away," Skiffington said. "They said it was leukemia. She's got cancer; she's going to die, she'll start suffering."

So she was euthanized.

Skiffington returned to Saratoga in 1987 and had a sensational afternoon early in the meet. He won one division of the Daryl's Joy Stakes with Persian Mews and finished second in the other with Mourjane, who had won the stakes the year before. "Two days later, Mourjane was shipping back home," Skiffington said. "He got colic really bad and died on the van to the veterinary hospital. One day, I'm one-two and the next day I'm dead." Mourjane, who had won 10 of 37 career starts in Europe and the United States and earned just under three quarters of a million dollars, was buried at Clare Court on the Saratoga backstretch.

Later in the 1987 meet, Skiffington won the Seneca Handicap with Palace Panther. A decade after that, Skiffington's outstanding grass mare Maxzene was the runner-up in the Eclipse Award voting for Top Female Turf Horse in 1997 and 1998.

Whether or not Allumeuse would have developed into

a stakes winner is impossible to know. "She had a very tragic ending," Skiffington said.

So did anyone who bet on her that August afternoon at Saratoga.

Jose Santos, 1987
(*Photo Courtesy of Barbara D. Livingston*)

CHAPTER 8

Lightning Strikes

Thunderstorms are as much a part of the Saratoga racing season as hand melons, the yearling sales and monumental upsets. Usually, the storms are intense, but brief in duration. Occasionally, the storms have caused delays during a race card. In 1984, a severe thunderstorm damaged some of the track's computer equipment. But races had never been canceled. Until 1986 and 1988.

Just five days after the Allumeuse disqualification, when fans might have thought they'd seen a once-in-a-lifetime event, they had to endure another. A savage thunderstorm, with lightning bolts hitting the ground at a furious rate, tore through Saratoga, Schenectady, Albany and Rensselaer Counties Thursday afternoon and evening, August 7, 1986. Saratoga actually was hit twice, initially by an afternoon storm with 35 to 40 miles per hour winds, and then again at 6:45 p.m. with a second torrential downpour.

Some 12,000 homes west and north of Albany lost power for an hour and there was massive flooding, particularly in Saratoga, where the rain, lightning and wind forced the first cancellation in Saratoga Race Course's 119-year history. Saratoga Harness canceled its evening program, as did the Philadelphia Orchestra, which was scheduled to perform that night at the Saratoga Performing Arts Center.

At Saratoga Race Course, which had been hit by rain in seven of the first eight days of the meet, the track was sloppy to begin with before a light rain began during the fourth race.

That was followed by heavy rain and bolts of lightning splitting the sky. The fifth race, a six furlong sprint, was reported to have gone off, but it was almost impossible to tell in the driving storm. "I have never in my life seen conditions as bad as they were today," jockey Robbie Davis said after winning the fifth on Columbus Circle. "It was coming down so hard. . . . It was like a monsoon. I really had to keep a hold on the horse because they were swimming in it. It was scary."

It was not a minority opinion. "I've been coming here for 27 years and this is the worst storm I have ever seen," trainer Laz Barrera said.

Jockey Jorge Velasquez agreed: "This is the absolute worst storm I have ever seen. This is no time to be working."

Following the fifth race, New York Racing Association President Gerard McKeon and the stewards pulled the plug on the remaining four races, including the Yaddo Stakes for New York-bred fillies and mares, which was re-scheduled. By then, pools of water had replaced the dirt in many spots on Saratoga's mile-and-an-eighth main track.

"During the running of the fifth race, the rain got quite heavy, and we were quite happy to see those horses get to the wire," Jockey Club Steward Dick McLaughlin said. "The horses just can't handle the track. They could stumble and fall."

Announcer Marshall Cassidy told the remaining crowd that races were canceled, and many fans had to wade through water up to their knees to reach their cars. "It wasn't fun to be a jockey today," Velasquez said. "It wasn't fun to be here today."

Yet track superintendent Joe King correctly predicted the resumption of racing the next day. "We're going to be fine," he said. "We'll be working on it into the night."

The 1988 storm was even worse, forcing the cancellation of a Grade 1 stakes, the John A. Morris Handicap (now named the Personal Ensign) for fillies and mares, on the next-to-last day of the meet.

The crowd of 35,953 at Saratoga, Sunday, August 28th, did, however, get to see a spectacular, if frightening, show. Heavy rain began at 5:20 p.m., 20 minutes before post time for the Morris, which had attracted a field of five. Then the storm got worse, just as the fillies began to saddle in the paddock.

Lightning bolts hit all over Saratoga Race Course, accompanied by hail and thunder as the rain became torrential.

Then a lightning bolt split a gigantic tree in the infield in half. There were downed limbs all over the main track.

Yet at 5:41 p.m., Cassidy announced that the rest of the card would be run. Four minutes later, he announced that the final two races were off.

"There were just two many ifs," McKeon said. "It wasn't a safe situation for anyone. We thought we might be able to get the races back on, but we sent an outrider and pony out on the track to see if the cushion had washed off, and it had. And the lightning was a big concern. We didn't want to take any chances."

McKeon's decision was a welcome one to the unfortunate horsemen and horses attempting to get ready for the Morris Handicap. "I was scared to death, I really was," Davis, the jockey on Ms. Eloise, said. "My whole insides were throbbing. I saw one horse running around, trying to get away from his walker. Could you imagine if that happened? My filly was running around and kicking and bucking. It just got worse and worse. I was very happy they canceled. With the lightning so close to the track, it's amazing no one got killed."

Jose Santos, scheduled to be aboard Rose's Cantina, said, "It was just too dangerous for the jockeys. And the horses were kicking and jumping . . . not too many of them like lightning. The animals were scared. Everybody was scared."

Clabber Girl's jockey, Angel Cordero, Jr., was one of them. "I certainly didn't want to ride in lightning," he said. "I hate lightning."

Clabber Girl's trainer D. Wayne Lukas said the decision

to cancel was the right one: "Of course, we would have liked to have gotten the race in because it was a Grade 1. You had to be concerned, though, with everyone standing in an open area like that."

Cassidy announced that fans who came back the next day would get free grandstand admission and a free program. He also told bettors that the Pick Six on races three through eight had to be condensed to a Pick Five. There were 21 correct Pick Five tickets, each worth $4,731.

NYRA decided to run the Morris Handicap as a non-betting race between Monday's fifth and sixth races.

But conditions on Monday were nearly as bad as Sunday: drenching rain and unseasonable cold which limited attendance to 13,261 despite free admission and a program on the closing day of the meet.

Four races scheduled for the turf never had a chance of remaining on grass as there were 38 late scratches. When six of the eight horses scratched from the second race, it became a match race for claimers.

Surprisingly, though, the track condition was tolerable. "It wasn't too bad," jockey Brian Peck told Keith Marder of the *Times Union*. "It's not as bad as I thought it would be."

Davis said, "The track is really getting a lot of water on top of it. It was really deep, but the horses seemed to be handling it well."

Regardless, LeRoy Jolley, the trainer of Roses Cantina, thought the Morris Handicap might be postponed again. "It looked like that earlier in the day," he said. "If the track was dangerous, the jocks would not want to ride. It was one of those situations where they had to make sure it was safe for everybody. It worked out good for me."

That's because his filly won the Morris Handicap by five lengths under Santos after Grecian Flight and Clabber Girl dueled themselves into defeat on the lead.

Seattle Meteor won the stakes originally scheduled for closing-day, the six furlong Spinaway Stakes, under Randy Romero. The two-year-old filly got six furlongs in 1:12 3/5, more than a tad off the brilliant Ruffian's stakes record 1:08 3/5 in 1974. Then again, the track Seattle Meteor raced on was more than a tad off.

Sean Clancy with Seminole Spirit
(*Photo Courtesy of Barbara D. Livingston*)

CHAPTER 9

Fall from Grace

In the first race at Saratoga, August 3, 1995, steeple-chase jockey Sean Clancy put new meaning into the concept of "holding on to the wire."

Clancy, who has moved on to become a successful journalist and author at the young age of 31, was riding Roberto's Grace, part of trainer Tom Voss's three horse entry, in a 2 1/16 mile steeplechase race for $20,000-$25,000 claimers.

If there is a person on the planet who enjoys Saratoga more than Clancy, he would be hard to find. Clancy authored "Saratoga Days, A Look Inside Racing's Greatest Meet," and cherished every mount he had at Saratoga, where steeplechase racing receives its greatest visibility.

Clancy is not alone in his appreciation. "Saratoga, to us, like everybody else, is the highlight of the year," Clancy's close friend and top rider, Chip Miller, said. "You want to win races at Saratoga. Nobody wanted to win more than Sean, and, at the time, he was having trouble winning races there. He worked his ass off, but he wasn't having a lot of success there."

Clancy, who led the country in victories in 1998, would retire at the end of 2002 with a record of five wins in 13 years at Saratoga, where there are only 12 steeplechase races for the whole meet. Still, each one carries purses which are gigantic compared to jump races at smaller venues the rest of the year.

So if you can get a ride in a $20,000 claimer, you take it, even if the horse is the weakest part of a three-horse entry. "He was the worst part," Clancy said.

And, despite the considerable success Voss has had over the years at Saratoga, bettors that afternoon weren't terribly impressed with his entry, sending the threesome, Bundle of Money, Lone Mountain and Roberto's Grace, off at 4.40-to-1 in the field of 12. A two-horse Jonathan Sheppard entry, Big Band Show and Amending, would go off the 9-5 favorite, and Hurler, ridden by Chip Miller, the 3.40-to-1 second choice.

Roberto's Grace was regally bred—a son of Roberto out of Wings of Grace, by Key to the Mint—but had little success on the flat, winning just one of 29 starts. For that matter, he had little success over jumps, either, finishing with two wins in 20 starts. But one of them had been in his first start in 1995, though he followed that with a did-not-finish and distant fifth before entering the starting gate at Saratoga.

It was an eventful race right from the start when Bundle of Money wheeled, refusing to race. Then Prenuptial fell over the first fence. Later, Amending, who had the lead, went extremely wide and faded, finishing last of the horses who finished the race.

Roberto's Grace, meanwhile, had worked out a dream trip under Clancy. "The race itself was perfect," Clancy said. "Nothing went wrong the whole way. The horse got up the inside. When I came to the last fence, he was three or four lengths in front. He really stretched over the last fence. I could feel him as he jumped the fence."

But when Roberto's Grace landed over that last jump, Clancy felt something else: "When he landed, that was the first time I had any indication anything was wrong."

Clancy realized that when he went to change his hold on his reins. "As soon as you land, you change your hold," Clancy said. "When I went to change my hold, I had the cross in my left and the stick in my right. The knot flew up and hit me in the head. I missed my cross. It's like brushing your teeth. I went and missed it again. The knot was in the way.

That's when I realized something was wrong. It was right after the last fence, about at the eighth pole."

Roberto's Grace's saddle was slipping. That's an unusual, but certainly not an unprecedented development during a race. In the 1978 Jockey Club Gold Cup against Exceller and Seattle Slew, Affirmed's saddle slipped and he finished a distant fifth, the only time he was out of the money in 29 career starts.

Of course, the degree of slippage is vital. So is the timing. If it's right after the start, it's hopeless. If it's near the end, it may not be.

"We had made five strides away from the last fence," Clancy said. "I made a conscious decision. I said, 'How far can the saddle go?' I've had plenty of saddles slip. I figured I'd just keep riding to the finish. And that was working fine. Until he propped when the saddle got real far back. He bucked like a buckin' bronco. He half-kicked me in the air. I was fine until then."

Certainly not afterwards. "I lost my balance," Clancy said. "He was going to the right. I was trying to keep him straight. Then it fell apart."

That's when Clancy made the dangerous decision to hold on to Roberto's Grace's neck until the finish line.

Miller, riding Hurler, was behind Roberto's Grace as this was unfolding. And he could not believe what he was seeing. "The last 50 yards, I was a spectator," Miller said. "You just don't see things like that happen, especially at Saratoga. He had it won. He was a lock. You go two miles and jump over all those fences and then your saddle slips 50 yards from the wire. It was unbelievable."

And it was happening right in front of the crowd, who quickly realized two things: Roberto's Grace was trying to hold on to the lead, which was shrinking with every mis-stride, and Clancy was trying to hold on to his horse's neck until the finish line.

Miller was proud of his buddy for trying. "He rode to win," Miller said. "You don't worry about being safe. You ride for two miles and jump over fences and you want to win. That's what Sean did. He didn't worry about getting hurt."

Clancy almost pulled it off.

Just before the wire, Big Band Show was almost even with Roberto's Grace and Clancy was still on his horse.

The two horses crossed the finish line together in a blur as Clancy fell to the ground, where he would be struck by another horse.

This had to be the first time in racing history that the photo finish would reveal not only the winning horse, but whether or not one of jockeys was still on top of him.

"It was a photo finish," Clancy said. "I thought we won."

He had not. Big Band Show had won by a nose, and, even if Roberto's Grace had won, he would have been disqualified for not carrying his weight, 140 pounds including Clancy, for the entire duration of the race. Roberto's Grace had finished second, three-quarters of a length ahead of Hurler, but was disqualified and placed last because the stewards ruled Clancy was not aboard at the finish line.

Voss was disappointed: "I thought he was still on the horse when he crossed the finish line," Voss said. "I didn't think he touched the ground."

The stewards disagreed. One of them, Clinton Pitts, said, "He did not carry his weight across the finish line. If his (Clancy's) feet would have been in the air, it would have been okay."

Clancy was not okay. Though he was coherent enough to tell Voss that he thought Roberto's Grace had suffered a heart attack or broken his leg—neither had happened—he was in considerable pain as he was helped off the track and into an ambulance.

"I had a little concussion," Clancy said. "I was slightly out of it. People were trying to talk to me and I couldn't figure out what they were saying. At the time, I still wasn't sure what happened."

The truth is that there is no concussion that is little, and that Clancy had or would have several concussions, leading him to retire from riding in 2000 and concentrate on his writing career. He and his brother, Joe, a former amateur rider and assistant trainer, started their own newspaper, The *Steeplechase Times*. Sean Clancy had already won an honorable mention in the 1997 Eclipse Award for magazine writing with a story he penned for The Blood-Horse. Undoubtedly, other books will follow "Saratoga Days." He has a limitless future in front of him.

And the past? Well, though he can laugh about that August afternoon on Roberto's Grace—"I have a good sense of humor," he said—he still is not at peace with not winning that race at his favorite track in the world. "My choice was to hold on for dear life, or, I was going to fall and definitely lose," he said. "So I figured, 'What the hell?' I wanted to win. I kept riding.

"The bitch of it all is that, as a jump jockey, you don't get that many opportunities to ride in a race at Saratoga. Basically, you have 12 chances to ride. To win a race at Saratoga is very special. I just missed on a winner at Saratoga."

Not by much.

Chris McCarron
(Photo Courtesy of Adam Coglianese)

CHAPTER 10

California Dreamers

When Hall of Fame jockey Chris McCarron retired after winning the Affirmed Handicap at Hollywood Park on Came Home, June 23, 2002, he had won just about every major stakes race in North America, including five Breeders' Cup Classics and two Kentucky Derbies. He'd ridden three Horses of the Year, John Henry, Alysheba and Tiznow, and was sixth all-time in wins (7,141) and first in earnings ($264 million), though his earnings mark has already been toppled by Pat Day. McCarron won the Eclipse Award for Apprentice Jockey in 1974 and the Eclipse Award for Outstanding Jockey six years later.

"The one regret that I had retiring is that I didn't get to ride at Saratoga for an entire meet," McCarron, now the General Manager at Santa Anita, said in November 2003. "We had Del Mar (in San Diego). I wish I had ridden at Saratoga for one full summer, because it's probably looked at as the most prestigious meet in the country."

Even so, McCarron won many Saratoga stakes: the Adirondack, Go for Wand, Honorable Miss, Hopeful (on Came Home), Jim Dandy, King's Bishop, Sanford, Schuylerville, Sword Dancer and the Travers. Not bad for a kid from Dorchester, Massachusetts, who made Southern California his permanent base in 1978.

McCarron won his first Travers by a nose when Forty
Niner out gamed Seeking the Gold and Pat Day in 1988, and
his second three years later when Corporate Report won the
Mid-Summer Derby by a neck over Preakness Stakes and
Belmont Stakes winner Hansel, who suffered a career-ending
injury in the race, but still finished second in a courageous performance.

In 1997, McCarron picked up a mount for the Travers
on Deputy Commander for California trainer Wally Dollase.
McCarron had almost gotten killed riding against Deputy
Commander, who was ridden by Corey Nakatani, a month ear-
lier in the $500,000 Swaps Stakes at Hollywood Park. Corey
Nakatani rode Deputy Commander.

McCarron was aboard Hello, who had won five of 13
starts and $473,919 heading into the Swaps, July 20th. But at
roughly the same time Free House, the 2-5 favorite in the
Swaps, took command of the race on the way to a 3 1/2 length
win over Deputy Commander in a fast 1:45.80 for the mile and
an eighth, Hello, racing in fifth, broke down. Hello had suffered a compound fracture of his left front leg and was euthanized. McCarron was thrown clear of his horse, but injured his
left shoulder. Though it wasn't fractured, McCarron was
forced to take off his mounts the rest of the afternoon and
could only watch as two of them, Marlin and Twice the Vice,
both morning line favorites, won two $400,000 stakes, the
Grade 1 Vanity Handicap and the Grade 2 Sunset Handicap,
respectively. What could possibly make up for that?

Free House had been magnificent in his six battles with
Silver Charm earlier that year. After losing to him by a length
and three-quarters in the San Vicente, he'd beaten Silver
Charm by three-quarters of a length in the San Felipe and by a
head in the Santa Anita Derby. Silver Charm exacted revenge
in the Triple Crown. Silver Charm won the Kentucky Derby by
a head over Captain Bodgit with Free House another 3 1/2
lengths back in third. The 1997 Preakness was one of the greatest races in Triple Crown history, Silver Charm edging Free
House by a head with Captain Bodgit just another head

behind. In the Belmont Stakes, Touch Gold denied Silver Charm the first Triple Crown in 19 years by three-quarters of a length in the Belmont Stakes, with Free House another length behind in third, 14 lengths ahead the rest of the field.

But Silver Charm would not return to the races until late December. Touch Gold and Free House were pointing to the Travers. Neither one made it.

Though he had never started a horse at Saratoga, trainer Wally Dollase had been to Saratoga many times.

A native of Fort Atkinson, Wisconsin, Dollase worked for trainers Buster Millerick and Noble Threewitt before going on his own and winning with his first starter, My Thief, at Bay Meadows in 1967.

Dollase made a career change, and managed a breeding farm, Rancho Rio Vista in Atascadero, California, from 1969 to 1984, when he returned to the track to train.

"When I had the breeding farm, after the end of the breeding season, June 15th, we'd go to Royal Ascot (in England)," Dollase said. "And then, a month later, we always went to Saratoga and Lake George. I saw a lot of great races there. Affirmed and Alydar. That was a big deal for me to see horses like that. That's one reason my kids are in it (racing)."

Dollase's son, Craig, became a trainer and has his own stable. Craig's sister, Aimee, assists her father and also trains a couple horses on her own. Their sister, Michelle, runs a lay-up facility for injured horses in Bradbury, California. Of his four children, only Carrie, a nurse, is not involved directly with horses. Dollase's wife Cindy handles the stable's books.

Dollase developed 1990 Champion Turf Horse Itsallgreektome, and 1996 Champion Older Filly Jewel Princess.

Deputy Commander was a dark bay son of Deputy Minister out of the outstanding grass mare Anka Germania, a daughter of Malinowski who won more than $900,000 from 16 career victories. Deputy Commander was unraced at two, but

he more than made up for it at three and would eclipse Silver
Charm, Touch Gold and Free House as 1997s leading three-
year-old earner.

After winning a maiden race by four lengths at Santa
Anita in his third career start, Deputy Commander finished
fifth in the Arkansas Derby and third in the Crown Royal
American Stakes in his lone start on grass. Dollase returned
his colt to dirt, and he won the Grade 3 Affirmed Handicap by
two lengths before finishing second to Free House in the
Swaps Stakes.

Dollase pointed Deputy Commander to the Grade 1
$400,000 Secretariat Stakes on turf at Arlington Park in
Chicago, August 24th, the day after the $750,000 Grade 1
Travers. Even when it became apparent Silver Charm and Free
House would not enter the Travers, Dollase stuck to his plan.
But when word came out that a recurring foot problem would
keep Touch Gold out of the Travers, too, Dollase decided he
would start his first horse at Saratoga Race Course. In the
Travers.

That was not the only change Dollase made with
Deputy Commander. He would get a new rider, Chris
McCarron, who would have ridden Touch Gold, another son of
Deputy Minister, in the Travers. Dollase also decided to
remove the blinkers Deputy Commander had worn in his six
previous starts. "They were due to come off," Dollase
explained to Dave Grening in *Thoroughbred Times*. "This colt is
green. You could see how he acted in the paddock with the
crowd around him. He can't do anything but get better. If he
starts conserving his energy, which he's not doing, he could be
a very special horse."

The horse Deputy Commander had to beat in the
Travers was Behrens, trained by Jim Bond, whose presence in
Saratoga's signature stakes the year before was just as unlikely
as Dollase's. Bond galloped horses for his dad, a trainer, when
he was 11. He got his trainer's license five years later, worked
six months for Noel Hickey, then struck out on his own. He
almost didn't make it.

From 1976 through 1987, Bond barely carved out a career at Finger Lakes, winning a total of 76 races and never earning more than $51,187 in a single season. In 1987, he saddled one winner from 25 starters and made $6,244.

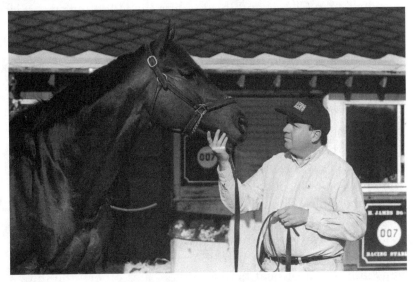

Jim Bond and Behrens, 1998
(*Photo Courtesy of Barbara D. Livingston*)

But he also made a connection which changed his life. After hearing that Virginia Kraft Payson, who owned the Payson Park Training Center, was looking for a trainer, Bond sent her a letter and resume, selling her on the idea of racing some of her New York-breds at Finger Lakes. At nearly the same time, Donald and Anne Rudder, who comprise Rudlein Stable, also sent Bond horses.

Payson provided Bond with his break-out horse, her homebred L'Carriere, a New York-bred by 1984 Travers winner Carr de Naskra. Unsatisfied with the horse's progress under trainer Roger Attfield, she gave Bond a shot and he made the most of it. "He's the horse that jumped out and caught the world," Bond said. "He was an incredible horse. I had always had horses for her, but I never had her 'A' string."

Bond got L'Carriere in mid-spring of his four-year-old

season. "He was lightning in a bottle," Bond said. "He flourished."

L'Carriere won the Grade 3 1995 Saratoga Cup Handicap, then finished second to Cigar in the $3 million Breeders' Cup Classic and third to him the following spring in the inaugural $4 million Dubai World Cup. "It was a great run," Bond said.

Others would follow.

Will's Way would take him to the 1996 Travers and win. "The year before Will's Way won, nobody knew my name," Bond said. "A kid from the Finger Lakes, what's he doing putting a horse in the Travers?"

Partners William Clifton, Jr., and Rudlein Stable purchased Will's Way, a son of Easy Goer, out of Willamae, by Tentam, for $95,000 as a yearling at the 1994 Keeneland September Sale. Though he trained sharply as a two-year-old, Will's Way had nagging minor problems and Bond decided to delay Will's Way's debut until his three-year-old season. "He was a colt we couldn't push," Bond said. "He had tiny problems, a little bit of heat here and there and other little things that tell you, if you go on, you're going to have a bigger problem. The clients I have are very good and patient. A lot of other trainers don't have the clientele who can say it's worth waiting. If you have enough patience, it can reward you a majority of the time. Probably, what's a little wrong with our business is that everybody is after the fast buck. If you look at older horses, you see four and five-horse fields going for a lot of money. What good is the investment if the horse breaks down? Will's Way had to mature."

Will's Way matured quickly, winning his debut, February 10, 1996, by 2 1/4 lengths at Gulfstream Park, then an allowance race. He suffered a muscle tear—apparently when he finished third in the $200,000 Flamingo Stakes at Hialeah—and Bond decided to point him to the Travers. After winning an allowance race at Belmont Park, Will's Way dueled the length of the stretch with Preakness Stakes winner Louis Quatorze in the $150,000 Jim Dandy Stakes. Racing on Will's

Way's outside, Louis Quatorze prevailed by a neck. It was 15 lengths back to Secreto de Estado in third. In the Travers, Will's Way dueled on Louis Quatorze's outside through the stretch and wore him down to take the Travers by three-quarters of a length. Haskell Stakes winner Skip Away, the 7-5 favorite, was third, and Belmont Stakes winner Editor's Note fourth.

The following afternoon, L'Carriere won the Saratoga Cup Handicap. The kid from Finger Lakes had arrived.

He hoped he had another Travers winner in his barn, Clifton and Rudlein Stable's Behrens, a son of 1981 Kentucky Derby and Preakness winner Pleasant Colony they purchased for $225,000 at the 1995 Keeneland July Yearling Sale. The path he took to the Travers was nearly identical to Will's Way's. Behrens was unraced at two, and won his debut by 4 3/4 lengths at three at Gulfstream Park, January 18, 1997, under Jerry Bailey, who would ride Behrens in his first seven starts. Behrens, however, came out of his initial race with a fracture in his left ankle. He made quick progress after surgery and returned to the races, May 24th, winning an allowance race at Belmont Park.

Making only his third lifetime start, Behrens won the Grade 2 Dwyer Stakes at Belmont Park by a length and a quarter. He was heading for the Travers and would prep in the Jim Dandy, the path Will's Way had traveled. "Behrens was almost a ditto," Bond said.

Then Behrens, like Will's Way, lost in the Jim Dandy, finishing fourth, 4 3/4 lengths behind Touch Gold's stablemate, Awesome Again, on a sloppy track after a horrendous trip. The Daily Racing Form comment was "Broke awkwardly, steadied, lacked room 16th pole." Bond said, "He got bounced around there. He didn't have the seasoning to deal with it. It was circumstances."

One of those circumstances was the sloppy track Behrens was racing on for the first time. Was that part of the problem?

And what would happen if the track came up sloppy for the Travers 20 days later?

Nineteen days later, just after the final race on the day before the Travers, one of those vicious thunderstorms which habitually roar through Saratoga came calling.

There was hail nearly the size of golf balls, accompanied by lightning, thunder and a torrential downpour. How could the track be anything but sloppy for the 128th running of the Travers?

Chris McCarron was playing golf in California on Tuesday, four days before the Travers, when he got the call. His mother, Helen, had succumbed to brain cancer at the age of 74. "I was playing golf in Rancho Santa Fe," McCarron said. "I got on a plane that night and flew home to Boston."

There, he, his dad, his five brothers and three sisters tried dealing with their grief. "We had a wake for my mother on Thursday and the funeral on Friday," McCarron said. "I was basically just ready to cancel the trip to Saratoga. My five brothers, three sisters and my dad all convinced me that she would not have wanted me to miss the race. I'm really sure, there's no doubt in my mind, that that's what she wanted. I don't have any regrets."

Even so, McCarron wondered what the track condition would be for the Travers. "I was aware that there was serious weather going through there," McCarron said. "I was hopeful that if the track was going to come up sloppy, that Wally wouldn't scratch. And, secondly, that Deputy Commander would handle it."

He would. So would Behrens.

The person their connections could thank was track superintendent Don Orlando.

Orlando grew up in Ozone Park in the shadow of Aqueduct Racetrack, but he never went there until he finished his stint in the Army at the age of 21. Orlando's younger brother, Michael, got a job with NYRA in track maintenance in June 1960. That September, Michael heard of an opening there. He called his brother and asked, "Do you want to come down?"

His brother said, 'yes,' and Don Orlando began working for the New York Racing Association on September 12,

1960. A year later, there was an opening with track superintendent Dick Strickland. Orlando got the job and spent the next 41 years working on the tracks at Aqueduct, Belmont Park and Saratoga Race Course.

At Aqueduct, there was a laboratory at the end of the grandstand. "We tested the cushion (of the track), different sands from each track," Orlando said. "Once a month, we took samples from all the tracks and did tests to make sure they weren't getting too sandy."

When Strickland retired, Joe King became NYRA's track superintendent in the late 1960s. He made Orlando his foreman, then his assistant. "I learned from the best," Orlando said.

When Joe King retired at the end of 1993, Orlando became track superintendent, a position he kept until he retired in 2001.

If there is a defining moment in each person's career, Orlando's came sometime between the late afternoon of August 22nd and the first race the following day at Saratoga Race Course after a malevolent thunderstorm and accompanying giant hail tattooed the racetrack without mercy. "That was unbelievable," Orlando said. "It started pouring so hard. That was a tremendous amount of rain, two to three inches of rain, probably in less than an hour and a half. And it was hailing like crazy."

Then it stopped, and Orlando and his crew went to work.

"As soon as the last race was done, we sealed the track," Orlando said. "We took the wooden floats that we have, and then we went over it with the steel plates to pack it down. You're taking the ridges (on the track) down, compacting it, so that you're not sinking."

"We wanted to do that so the water would flow across the track and keep some of the water from coming in. We just made it. I went home that night, took a quick shower and came back. I got back to the track at about eight o'clock. I walked around the racetrack just to see it. I was very happy with it. I said, 'Look at this; we're going to get lucky.'"

Orlando and his crew returned at 4 .a.m. the morning of the Travers. "We went around the track with shovels and bled whatever water was left on it to run off, just to get the water off the racetrack," Orlando said.

The next step was to close the main track for training that morning. "If you let a horse train, you'll get a little saucer every time a horse's hoof goes down," Orlando said. "Instead of water flowing off, it goes into that little saucer. Then you can't get it off the track."

NYRA President Terry Meyocks arrived at 6 a.m. "He said, 'What do you think?'" Orlando recounted. "I said, 'I think it might be fast.'"

Orlando had an ally he had not counted on. "We did everything we could, but Mother Nature helped," Orlando said. "It rained so hard that it actually packed it down. The water didn't have much of a chance to get onto the track. We cut it very lightly and checked it again," Orlando said. "It was a nice sunny day. There was a breeze. So we were pleasantly surprised. We were fast by the first or second race."

Orlando got a letter from Meyocks expressing his deep appreciation to Orlando and his staff for their work before the Travers "under very difficult circumstances."

The bottom line to Orlando, however, was the same one he used for every race: "We had a good day. Everybody came home safe."

On Saturday morning, McCarron boarded a flight at Logan Airport in Boston and headed for Saratoga hoping to become just the seventh jockey to win three Travers Stakes in his career. So was Bailey, who'd won the Mid-Summer Derby in 1986 on Wise Times and in 1993 on Kentucky Derby winner Sea Hero.

Bond, meanwhile, was trying to become only the fifth trainer to win back-to-back Travers. Dollase was sending out his first Saratoga starter.

The connections of the other six horses in the Travers' field of eight had other aspirations. Stronach Stable's

Awesome Again, trained by California-based David Hofmans, was searching for some respect. Though he had won the Jim Dandy by three lengths, few people placed him in the same category as his stable-mate, Touch Gold. Stronach owned 75 percent of the colt and Robert and Janice McNair's Stonerside Farm the other 25.

Hofmans and Frank Stronach didn't see Awesome Again's Jim Dandy Stakes victory, because they were at Monmouth Park in New Jersey that very afternoon watching McCarron ride Touch Gold to a 1 1/4 length victory over Anet in the $1.24 million Haskell Invitational Handicap. Free House was third. Because there were two Grade 1 stakes winners in the field, Stronach and the McNair's received a $250,000 bonus, upping Touch Gold's Haskell payday to $850,000. The entire purse for the Jim Dandy was $350,000. A patch over Touch Gold's quarter crack in his left front foot—a persistent problem much of his three-year-old season—apparently did the job in the Haskell. But Touch Gold would still miss the Travers because of it and make just 15 career starts.

Albert Fried, Jr.'s Affirmed Success—like Awesome Again, who would win the 1998 Whitney Handicap and 1998 Breeders' Cup Classic—would accomplish greater feats later in his career, winning multiple stakes including the 2002 Grade 1 Carter Handicap at the age of nine.

Neither Awesome Again, sent off the 1.45-to-1 favorite, Affirmed Success, nor longshots Blazing Sword, Cryptocloser, Twin Spires and Affairwithpeaches would make an impact that afternoon at Saratoga.

The 1997 Travers was a two-horse race.

After arriving in Saratoga, McCarron struggled to keep his focus on the Travers as he waited in the jockey's room. "It was very different," McCarron said. "I was pretty quiet. I was still confused at that point. I was just hoping that I was doing the right thing. One thing I didn't want to happen was to be so distracted that I would detract from Deputy Commander's chance of winning. I take my job very seriously. It's hard to out-perform Bailey or Pat Day even when you're 100 percent."

Bailey said he, like many others in the jockeys' room, was not aware of McCarron's mother's passing. Bailey and Behrens would be the 2.45-to-1 second choice in the wagering. Deputy Commander was the 4-1 third choice of a crowd of 46,532.

McCarron was relieved to see the condition of the track by mid-afternoon. "The maintenance crew did a wonderful job," McCarron said. "I was surprised that it was a fast track. It started out pretty wet, but there was a good breeze that day and it helped dry it out."

In the paddock before the Travers, Dollase spoke with McCarron. "It was very emotional in the paddock," Dollase said. "I even asked him before the race. I said, 'You don't have to do this.' He said to me, 'My mother would want me to.'"

Dollase didn't say much after that. "Wally just told me how big and strong the colt was, and that he had taken blinkers off," McCarron said. "In his previous races, he was pulling pretty hard on Corey (Nakatani). The key was to get him to relax. Nurse him along. He said, 'He'll finish better if you conserve that energy.'"

That's exactly what McCarron did.

While Affirmed Success and Twin Spires, a last-second addition to the field by trainer D. Wayne Lukas, battled head-to-head on the lead the first three-quarters of a mile, Deputy Commander stalked in third. "I was very pleased with the way he relaxed," McCarron said. "He wasn't pulling me at all." Behrens and Awesome Again raced in tandem, fourth and fifth.

Affirmed Success finally put away Twin Spires to lead briefly on the final turn, but Deputy Commander stormed past him powerfully at the top of the stretch. Bailey said, 'Go,' on Behrens and he accelerated quickly to engage Deputy Commander at the eighth pole.

Then they went at it nose-to-nose for the final eighth of a mile, Deputy Commander and McCarron in the red and green silks and red cap of Mandysland Farms on the inside and Behrens and Bailey in the purple silks and purple cap of

Rudlein Stable and Clifton alongside.

Neither horse gave an inch.

Neither rider conceded an inch, McCarron using his whip left-handed and Bailey using his whip right-handed.

"When I hit him left-handed, he gave me more," McCarron said. "I was pretty confident that he had enough left to hold off Behrens."

Behrens looked like he might prevail 100 yards from the wire, but Deputy Commander was absolutely resolute. They crossed the finish line together, Deputy Commander perhaps a nose in front. "I was pretty sure I had won," McCarron said. Bailey said, "Sometimes you have a feeling that you won. I didn't have a feeling one way or another, so that was a bad sign."

Watching from a box in the clubhouse, Dollase couldn't tell. "They hooked up at the top of the stretch," Dollase said. "It seems like that happens a lot in the Travers. It was head and head. From my angle, I wasn't sure if we won or not. All these partners in the horse, they came screaming out of the grandstand. I had to stop them before they went to the winner's circle because how could you be sure?"

Deputy Commander had won by a nose. Behrens had finished second, seven lengths ahead of Awesome Again in third.

Bond thought he had the race won. "Jerry Bailey was aboard; I just thought for sure that we had enough in the tank to get by," Bond said. "He had him, but Deputy Commander came back. It was head bobs for the last 70 yards. It hurt bad, just because we got the taste of winning the year before. It was sickening. That was my hardest defeat. It burned a hole in me, and that hole will be there for the rest of my life. I thought Behrens was the best horse."

Not this day.

McCarron was all right until he got back to the winner's circle. "I saw Cindy Dollase, Wally's wife, crying," McCarron said. "That's when I lost it."

Dollase remembers. "They presented the trophy; that's

when he broke down," Dollase said. "Then, as they always do, they take you to an interview room with 15 or 20 press people there. Then he really broke down. He was very emotional. I felt bad for Chris's mom, but I felt the race kind of soothed him and helped him get through the day."

Almost forgotten was Dollase's immense accomplishment. He had won the Travers Stakes with the first horse he ever saddled at Saratoga. "I was so fortunate to be able to do that," he said six years later. "To win the Travers after going up there summer after summer with the kids. I knew how prestigious it was. And Behrens was a very special horse."

Behrens would prove exactly that, burying Touch Gold when he won the Grade 2 Pegasus Handicap at The Meadowlands by 5 3/4 lengths in his very next start after the Travers. Six hours earlier, Will's Way had suffered a career ending injury in the Woodward Stakes at Belmont Park.

While Behrens nearly gave Bond back-to-back Travers, New York-bred longshot Raffie's Majesty nearly gave him two in three years, finishing third in the 1998 Mid-Summer Derby in a three-horse photo. Coronado's Quest beat Victory Gallop by a nose and Raffie's Majesty was just another nose behind.

But Bond had yet another photo finish Saratoga stakes loss to endure.

Though he was winless in four starts as a four-year-old, Behrens returned at five to win four consecutive graded stakes, the Grade 1 Gulfstream Park and Oaklawn Handicaps and the Grade 2 Mass Cap and Suburban Stakes. He brought that four race win streak to Saratoga in 1999 and finished second by a nose to Victory Gallop in the Grade 1 Whitney Handicap after a stretch-long battle not much different from the 1997 Travers. Behrens retired with nine wins, eight seconds and three thirds in 27 career starts and earnings of $4,563,500.

Bond still has trouble discussing his near Travers double. "It would have been nice to win two in a row," Bond said. "That was probably the biggest heartache of all. I pray to God that I can win another one."

Bond and his wife, Tina Marie, watched the 1997

Travers replay that night. "My wife said to me, 'Maybe some-body needed it more. Maybe Chris needed that uplifting to get on with his whole life,'" Bond said. "She was probably right, but at that point of time, it was hard to get through my thick skull. He lost by a lip."

Wally Dollase
(*Photo Courtesy of the Schenectady Daily Gazette*)

Jerry Bailey, 2002
(*Photo Courtesy of Barbara D. Livingston*)

Chapter 11

The End of the World

Other thunderstorms lashing Saratoga Race Course over the last 30 years have been more damaging, but absolutely none were more sinister than the one that arrived in the late afternoon of September 2, 2000.

Most Saratoga thunderstorms are quick movers: they roar in, do their damage and leave. Not this one. This time, an immense, steel-gray cloud enveloped Saratoga Race Course in darkness and just sat there, almost like the mother ship in the film "Independence Day."

As the thunder roared, the lights on the tote board went dark, then came back on. All power at the track was lost momentarily. The rain started to come in sheets, accompanied by a barrage of spectacular lightning bolts.

It was a hell of a backdrop for the 11 two-year-olds about to race in the $200,000 Grade 1 Hopeful Stakes. It looked like the end of the world.

No horse likes lightning or thunder, but at least older horses may have experienced such frightening circumstances earlier in their lives. Not these babies in their first season of racing, running in the most important race of their brief careers.

That's what made the 96th running of the Hopeful Stakes even more remarkable.

Not many Grade 1 stakes end in a dead heat, let alone a near triple dead-heat. This one did, as a colt who cost $1.9 million, and one who cost $9,000 and was chasing history, crossed the finish line together. The horse in between them, who only lost by a neck, would go on to win the Breeders' Cup Juvenile.

Of course, nobody knew any of this as the cloud of disaster moved over Saratoga Race Course. The New York Racing Association took the unusual step of sacrificing five minutes of betting by moving up post time by five minutes to try to get the Hopeful in before the storm got even worse. All that meant was that the two-year-olds would be denied a chance to warm-up as they normally would after the post parade.

There was nothing resembling normal that afternoon.

City Zip, purchased for $9,000 as a yearling because of a crooked leg, was seeking to become only the fourth horse to sweep Saratoga's three two-year-old stakes, the Sanford, Saratoga Special and Hopeful. Only Regret, who won all three in 1914 before becoming the first filly to win the Kentucky Derby the following spring, Campfire in 1916 and Dehere, who became Juvenile Champion in 1993, had swept the three stakes, a feat no longer possible since the New York Racing Association decided to stop running the Saratoga Special in 2004 (Native Dancer swept four two-year-old stakes at Saratoga in 1952, the Flash, Saratoga Special, Grand Union Hotel and Hopeful).

Linda Rice had replaced James Chapman as City Zip's trainer after his first three starts, a second by a head and 6 3/4 length win in maiden company and a second by half a length to the outstanding filly Gold Mover in the Grade 3 Kentucky Breeders' Cup Stakes.

City Zip flourished under Rice's care. After running third to Yonaguska in the Flash Stakes at Belmont Park, City Zip won three straight stakes, the Grade 3 Tremont at Belmont by 2 3/4 lengths, the Sanford at Saratoga by 3 1/2 lengths over Yonaguska, and the Saratoga Special by 2 1/4 lengths under Jose Santos, City Zip's rider once Rice took over. Whether or not the son of the brilliant speed sire Carson City could stretch out from the 6 1/2 furlongs of the Saratoga Special to the seven furlongs of the Hopeful was a legitimate concern. Rice obviously thought he could.

Michael Tabor's Yonaguska had little in common with City Zip other than their age. A $1.95 million purchase as a two-year-old in February 2000, Yonaguska had won his debut by 9 1/4 lengths at Churchill Downs for trainer D. Wayne Lukas and jockey Jerry Bailey. The son of Cherokee Run followed that impressive performance by taking the Flash Stakes by 2 1/2 lengths, but in the Sanford, he led late before tiring to second behind City Zip as the 1-2 favorite.

While Lukas had been dominant in the Hopeful—winning four of the previous 10 runnings—his 2000 Saratoga meet was a disaster. Lukas had lost 35 straight races before winning a race earlier on the September 2nd card, making him two-for-45 for the meet. City Zip had as many wins as Lukas.

There were other major players in the Hopeful field, including Stronach Stable's Macho Uno, a son of 1994 Horse of the Year Holy Bull trained by Joe Orseno and ridden by Edgar Prado. In his debut at Saratoga, Macho Uno had won a maiden race by 2 3/4 lengths easily as the 3-5 favorite.

Saint Verre had been even more impressive in his lone start, winning a maiden race at Philadelphia Park by 10 3/4 lengths as the 2-5 favorite in the incredibly fast time of 1:02 3/5 for 5 1/2 furlongs, 1 4/5 seconds faster than Macho Uno's win at Saratoga. Initially trained by Mary Goodman, Saint Verre was now in Shug McGaughey's barn. He would eventually wind up in the hands of Hall of Fame trainer Allen Jerkens and earn more than $400,000.

Scorpion, also trained by Lukas, but for other owners, had chased City Zip in three straight stakes, finishing second, third and second. He would return to Saratoga as a three-year-old in 2001 and defeat heavily-favored Congaree in the Jim Dandy Stakes.

Evening Attire was stepping up to stakes company off a nose maiden win at Saratoga. All he would do is win $1.8

million in a career still going strongly through the end of 2004.

There was a ton of quality in this Hopeful field, but the bottom line was how these two-year-olds would react to the frightening weather around them.

Yonaguska was an absolute handful in the paddock. "The weather stirred him up a lot," Lukas said.

Macho Uno tossed his head in the starting gate, bloodying Prado's nose.

City Zip didn't handle the streaks of lightning well. "Every time the sky would light up, he would look around and get startled," Santos said.

City Zip went off the 7-5 favorite in the field of 11 with Yonaguska 7-2, Saint Verre 4-1, Evening Attire 7-1 and Macho Uno 9-1. All the others were double-digit odds.

City Zip broke sharply, typical of his early speed, but uncharacteristically fell back to seventh as 66-1 longshot T P Louie took the lead and Yonaguska moved inside of him.

Yonaguska moved to the lead and seemed to have command of the race, even as Macho Uno, who had been between horses on the backstretch, got loose and advanced five wide on the turn.

Then Yonaguska's saddle slipped as Bailey tried to keep him together to the wire.

City Zip didn't appear to have a chance. Even as he began to rally, City Zip was behind Macho Uno, forcing Santos to take City Zip even wider on the turn. "At that point, I didn't think he had much chance," Rice said.

Nobody did. Yonaguska had a two length lead at the eighth pole, but Macho Uno and City Zip quickly closed the gap. In the final strides, Macho Uno, racing between Yonaguska and City Zip, tired as Yonaguska and City Zip hit the wire simultaneously.

Nobody—the fans, jockeys, trainers or owners—had a clue who had won the Hopeful. Both Bailey and Santos looked at the tote board for the answer as they quickly brought their horses back. They were forced to wait as the storm intensified.

Finally, Yonaguska's number '2' appeared first on the

tote board, then City Zip's '9' underneath it. But the red vertical line next to both numbers revealed that the Hopeful had ended in a dead heat.

Santos was thrilled. "He overcame a lot to win this," he said. "This horse made history this afternoon."

Saint Verre had finished fourth, 7 1/4 lengths behind Macho Uno in third.

Macho Uno made two more starts as a two-year-old, winning the Grey Breeders' Cup at Woodbine in Toronto by seven lengths, then beating Point Given by a nose in the Breeders' Cup Juvenile. Macho Uno would be named 2000 Champion Two-Year-Old Colt and go on to win more than $1.8 million in his career. Point Given would return at three to win the Santa Anita Derby, Preakness, Belmont Stakes, Haskell Invitational and, in his final career start, the Travers on the way to being named 2001 Three-Year-Old Champion and Horse of the Year.

City Zip returned to Saratoga in 2001 to win the Grade 2 Amsterdam Stakes. He retired with a record of nine wins in 23 starts and earnings of $818,225.

Yonaguska won two Grade 2 stakes, the Hutcheson and Fall Highweight Handicap, and the Grade 3 Sport Page Handicap at three, retiring with six wins from 18 starts and earnings of $536,355.

Together, City Zip, Yonaguska and Macho Uno put on a hell of a show in the 2000 Hopeful despite the weather. The world didn't end; the storm finally passed, and the trio of two-year-olds, as well as Evening Attire, Saint Verre and Scorpion, did quite well for themselves. But they and their connections will never forget that stormy afternoon at Saratoga.

Carson Hollow (left) and You (right)
battle in the 2002 Test.
(*Photo Courtesy of Barbara D. Livingston*)

CHAPTER 12

Nose Jobs

If you think about it, the dynamics of a close finish in a horse race is rather remarkable. Two 1,000-pound Thoroughbreds traveling 35 to 40 miles per hour for distances of a mile or longer arriving at the finish line so close to each other that the human eye cannot distinguish whose nose or head crossed the wire first.

If you are lucky, you get to see one of these races in person.

If you're really lucky, you get to see a major stakes race with such a finish.

But you had to blessed, really, if you were on hand for the 1962 Travers Stakes, when Jaipur and Ridan battled the entire mile and a quarter head-to-head with neither one giving ground. Jaipur won by a desperate nose in a race many believe to be one of the most exciting in Thoroughbred racing history.

Even so, that was one dramatic finish in a major stakes race.

On July 27, 2002, fans at Saratoga got to see two. Within one hour.

On July 27, 2002, it took longer to find out who had won two graded stakes at Saratoga than it had taken to run them.

"Those were two of the greatest stretch battles you could have," Hall of Fame jockey Jerry Bailey said.

Of course, his appreciation might be heightened by the fact that he won both of them, both for Hall of Fame trainer Bobby Frankel. Frankel said afterwards, "I'm blessed right now; I don't know why. God bless Jerry Bailey. I needed him in both those races."

At the time, Bailey, himself was astonished. "I've never had two, not like that," he said.

The $500,000 Grade 2 Diana Handicap, a mile and an eighth grass stakes for fillies and mares, attracted a field of nine. The 3-2 favorite was Green Hills Farm's Voodoo Dancer, who'd won eight of 12 starts on grass, including the Grade 3 Locust Grove Handicap at Churchill Downs at the same distance in her previous start. Christophe Clement trained the four-year-old filly, who would break from the outside nine post under Jose Santos.

Another four-year-old filly, Juddmonte Farm's Tates Creek, had posted five wins and two seconds in seven grass starts. She went off the 7-2 second choice, breaking from the rail under Bailey. She had another advantage over Voodoo Dancer besides post position. She'd be carrying 117 pounds, three less than that rival. In a race decided by the length of a finger, those three pounds could have made the difference.

Tates Creek broke first, but Bailey took her back as Snow Dance and Babae, who had beaten Tates Creek by a neck in the Just A Game Breeders' Cup Handicap at Belmont Park June 8th, disputed the lead through moderate fractions. Bailey had Tates Creek tucked away neatly on the inside in third with longshot Reina Blanca alongside. Santos, meanwhile, had guided Voodoo Dancer into excellent position, a stalking fifth with a clear run on the outside.

Babae eventually forged past Snow Dance to take the lead heading into the far turn while Bailey decisively split Snow Dance and a tiring Reina Blanca to engage Babae.

"I had a great trip, but she's the kind of filly that you

can use a couple of times to get position and hold your position," Bailey said afterwards. "It's not like she has one run from the back, which makes it easier for me. And I already had the one post, so I could count on, pretty much, a ground saving trip the whole way."

But Babae fought off Tates Creek stubbornly with Voodoo Dancer bearing down on both of them from the outside. Tates Creek finally took a narrow lead in mid-stretch, but soon had Voodoo Dancer in her face. They crossed the finish line simultaneously in a head-bobbing finish.

"Watching the head bob, I wasn't sure," Frankel said. "Then they slowed the replay down (to slow motion). It looked like she got the bob."

Neither Santos nor Bailey knew until they returned their horses to be unsaddled and Tates Creek's No. '1' appeared on the toteboard above Voodoo Dancer's No. '10.'

Bailey was justifiably proud of his filly, whom he was riding for just the second time: "She reached down turning for home and she gave it a little more, because that other filly, I think, maybe got a nostril in front of her at one point."

It wasn't at the decisive point: the wire.

"It's tough, because it's just a matter of what stride they're on as who's going to win," Bailey said. "I will say I've ridden the other mare. She tries hard. My filly tries hard. So you hate to see a loser. If there had to be one, I was glad it was her."

Who could have imagined an even tighter finish just an hour later?

Seven three-year-old fillies entered the $250,000 Grade 1 Test Stakes at seven furlongs. The two who would be favored were multiple stakes winner You, who had six wins and two seconds in 10 starts and was owned by Edmund A. Gann, trained by Frankel and ridden by Bailey, and undefeated Carson Hollow, a New York-bred whose two length victory in the open Grade 1 Prioress Stakes at Belmont Park July 6th induced Stronach Stables to purchase a 60 percent interest in the filly from Hemlock Hills Farm. John Velazquez would ride

Carson Hollow for trainer Richard Dutrow, Jr., as she tried for her sixth straight win.

You, breaking from the two post and carrying 123 pounds, went off the 4-5 favorite. Carson Hollow, carrying 120 pounds from the rail, went off the 5-2 second choice. They staged an epic battle of wills.

Under pressure from Bold World and Short Note, Carson Hollow set a sizzling pace of :21.60 for the first quarter of a mile and :44.27 for the half. You was fifth early, then got shuffled back to last. After nearly getting stopped in traffic. Bailey split horses and dove to the inside, where there was the narrowest of openings inside of Carson Hollow. It would get even narrower.

Bailey thought he had Carson Hollow measured: "At the eighth pole, I thought I could win by a head, but to his filly's credit, she dug back in again."

You was in the tightest of quarters, nearly brushing the rail as she battled shoulder to shoulder with Carson Hollow, who wasn't conceding an inch despite disputing the suicidal pace.

"The advantage is always with the outside horse because they don't feel intimidated," Bailey said.

The two fillies' strides were absolutely synchronized as they crossed the finish line together. Announcer Tom Durkin said, "It's too close to call in a race that doesn't deserve a loser."

Meanwhile, Bailey and Velazquez were trying to figure out which filly had won.

"Coming back, Jerry said to me, 'What do you think?'" Velazquez said afterwards. "I said, 'I don't know. It's close, but I thought you got the bob.' And that's what it was."

Just as in the Diana Handicap, Bailey wasn't sure if he'd finished first or second. "Neither race, did I have any idea if I won," he said.

Frankel thought he had been beaten. "I thought I lost it because you couldn't see her black nose (because she was on the inside). You could see the other filly's head. But then, when they showed the re-run, I thought maybe I had a chance.

It was so close. She had her head in the right place and Carson Hollow didn't."

Both fillies returned to be unsaddled to a roar of applause even before the order of finish was posted on the tote board. "I never felt so good losing a race," Dutrow said. "I'm so proud of her."

Three years later, Bailey said Velazquez did the exact right thing in the stretch. "Johnny came off the rail a little bit," Bailey said. "When he saw me coming through, he made it really tight, which is what a good rider should do. My filly never blinked. A lot of horses get intimidated. Very few have the courage to go through holes like that. Most of them aren't that determined. The last jump she stuck her head out. That was a great race."

There were two of them an hour apart. The memories will last for years.

Phil Johnson
(*Photo Courtesy of Adam Coglianese*)

CHAPTER 13

Thirty-Six and Counting

Hall of Fame trainer Phil "P. G." Johnson has been spending summer afternoons at Saratoga racing Thorough-breds for more than four decades. In doing so, he's compiled the unimaginable streak of winning at least one race there for the past 36 years, and for 40 of the 41 years he raced there since he first ventured from his native Chicago to race full time in New York in 1962.

He arrived at Saratoga anonymously in 1962, and was deep into his first meet when he won a $5,000 maiden claimer in the ninth race of August 20th with Admiral Bayard. Sent off at odds of 7-2, Admiral Bayard won by a length and a half under Bobby Ussery.

Until 2003, Johnson had never come to Saratoga with a "big horse." Volponi changed that, prompting Johnson to run him in the Grade 1 $750,000 Whitney Handicap. "I've never run a horse in the Whitney," Johnson said before the meet.

That was okay. Johnson had never trained the winner of a Breeders' Cup race—he'd only started two—until October 26, 2002, when he returned to Arlington Park in his hometown of Chicago and watched with delight as Volponi, his family's four-year-old home-bred, annihilated the best horses in the world, not only winning the $4 million Breeders' Cup Classic at odds of 43-1, but posting the largest winning margin in the race's 18-year history: 6 1/2 lengths. Johnson had reached the pinnacle of his career 17 days after his 77th birthday.

Phil Johnson's First Winner or Stakes Winner Each Season at Saratoga

Year	Date	Race	Winner	Jockey	Odds	Stakes
1962	Aug. 20	9th	Admiral Bayard	Bobby Ussery	3.50-to-1	
1964	Aug. 5	2nd	Tri Quest	Mike Venezia	9.80-to-1	
1965	Aug. 3	8th	Swim To Me	Sandino Hernandez	14.90-to-1	
1966	Aug. 8	1st	Her Grace	Davie Hidalgo	1.60-to-1	
1968	Aug. 2	9th	Dead Aim	Angel Cordero, Jr.	.80-t0-1	
1969	Aug. 7	2nd	All of a Sudden	Ron Turcotte	1.70-to-1	
1970	Aug. 4	1st	Owens Son	Ron Turcotte	5.50-to-1	
1971	Aug. 2	8th	Admirals Fate	Mike Venezia	5.10-to-1	
1972	Aug. 5	9th	Francois Premier	Mike Venezia	2.40-to-1 (e)	
1973	Aug. 16	8th	Jimminy Gosh	Ernie Cardone	2.80-to-1	
1974	July 30	8th	Real Meaning	Darryl Montoya	2.40-to-1	
1975	July 28	3rd	Dinky Pinky	Eddie Maple	.90-to-1	
1976	Aug. 2	6th	Rich As Croesus	Eddie Maple	2.00-to-1	
1977	Aug. 8	6th	Sibaritica	Steve Cauthen	5.80-to-1	
1978	July 31	5th	Naval Orange	Jean-Luc Samyn	3.20-to-1	
1979	Aug. 2	2nd	El Kel	Jean-Luc Samyn	2.30-to-1	
1980	July 30	5th	Hey Babe	Frank Lovato, Jr.	4.10-to-1	
1981	Aug. 21	8th	*Naskra's Breeze	Jean-Luc Samyn	12.20-to-1	West Point
1982	Aug. 10	1st	Rich Butterfly	Frank Alvarado	10.90-to-1	
1983	Aug. 8	7th	*Geraldine's Store	Jean-Luc Samyn	5.30-to-1	Diana
1984	Aug. 20	8th	*Possible Mate	Don MacBeth	2.40-to-1	Nijana
1985	Aug. 1	5th	What A Dance	Jean-Luc Samyn	.50-to-1	
1986	July 31	7th	Raft	Jean-Luc Samyn	1.50-to-1	
1987	Aug. 9	7th	Stardusk	Jean-Luc Samyn	2.10-to-1	
1988	Aug. 3	8th	*Maplejinsky	Angel Cordero, Jr.	4.00-to-1	Alabama
1989	Aug. 9	1st	Crafty Mommy	Chris Antley	1.70-to-1	
1990	Aug. 4	1st	Far Out Beast	Jose Santos	2.80-to-1	
1991	Aug. 1	3rd	Colchis Island	Angel Cordero, Jr.	1.80-to-1	
1992	July 29	1st	Kiri's Clown	Jean Cruguet	1.80-to-1	
1993	Aug. 5	9th	*A in Sociology	Chris Antley	13.70-to-1	Natl Museum
1994	Aug. 25	9th	*Excellent Tipper	Mike Luzzi	2.50-to-1	
1995	July 29	8th	*Kiri's Clown	Mike Luzzi	14.20-to-1	Sword Dancer
1996	July 29	9th	Orange Boven	Jean-Luc Samyn	2.70-to-1	
1997	July 23	3rd	Born Twice	Jean-Luc Samyn	2.50-to-1	
1998	Aug. 2	4th	Hawk's Ability	Aaron Gryder	28.50-to-1	
1999	July 29	5th	Wing Along	Mike Luzzi	14.90-to-1	
2000	July 29	5th	Keep It Holy	Shaun Bridgmohan	18.30-to-1	
2001	Aug. 22	6th	Offtheturf	Shaun Bridgmohan	9.20-to-1	
2002	Aug. 3	5th	Romp and Stomp	Victor Carrero	10.10-to-1	
2003	Aug. 15	1st	Micmaceuse	Jorge Chavez	1.40-to-1	

(*)—stakes race

Given that Johnson could have started his versatile son of Cryptoclearance, out of Prom Knight by Sir Harry Lewis, in the Breeders' Cup Mile on grass instead of the Classic only made the victory sweeter. One great decision.

So, too, Johnson's decision to restore blinkers after

Volponi raced his last five times without them. Two great choices.

And, that instead of freshening up Volponi, he raced him in the Meadowlands Cup Handicap, where he was a strong second by three-quarters of a length at 2-1 to Burning Roma, just 22 days before the biggest race of his career. That's a hat trick of vital training decisions.

Johnson is far too humble to crow about any of them, but he will readily tell you that he screwed up Volponi's appearance in the Travers Stakes at Saratoga the year before.

"That was bad judgment on my part," Johnson said.

Volponi's inclusion in the Travers was kind of a lark. Johnson was still recovering from prostate cancer and related problems which required surgery when Volponi won an allowance race early in the 2001 Saratoga meet by 13 1/2 lengths under new jockey Richard Migliore.

"I'd never ridden Richie a lot," Johnson said. "I was not feeling too well from surgery and I heard him in the winner's circle say to Karen (Johnson's daughter who writes for the Daily Racing Form), 'This is my Travers horse.'"

"That was the farthest thing from my mind," Johnson continued. "But the next morning when I got to the barn, Richie was already there. He was enthused. He was like a kid with a new toy. He said, 'If this horse runs in the Travers like he ran yesterday. . . .'"

So Johnson took a shot, as did other trainers when they took on Point Given in the Midsummer Derby. But Johnson will tell you that he did more than suffer a lapse in judgment by entering Volponi in the race.

"He had two works," Johnson said. "He went 1:12 2/5 in the first. Then, five days before the Travers, he worked 1:10 and two (two-fifths). That, right there, really cooked him. He's a three-year-old. He really wasn't mature. He was over-trained, and I should have backed off."

Volponi was never involved in the Travers, which turned out to be Horse of the Year Point Given's final victory in his final race. Volponi broke slowly and finished seventh by 16

1/2 lengths, easily the worst performance of his career. He had only been worse than fourth just one other time in 25 starts, a fifth in the Grade 3 Hawthorne Derby on grass earlier in 2001.

But there was no lasting damage from the Travers. Volponi returned to finish second by a nose in a non-winners of three races (two other than maiden, claiming or starter), then won in that class.

And then he took his game to a new level.

He shipped to New Jersey to win the Grade 2 Pegasus Handicap by 2 3/4 lengths over Burning Roma and concluded his three-year-old season by taking on older horses in the Grade 1 Cigar Mile. Sent off at 5-1 in a distinguished field of nine, Volponi was bumped at the start, but recovered to finish fourth, five lengths behind Left Bank, a blossoming star himself who would go on to be named Champion Older Male the following year, out-pointing Volponi.

Volponi had arrived, but the best was yet to come as he proved himself the most versatile, talented horse in North America in 2002, winning the Grade 3 Poker Handicap on grass and the Grade 1 Breeders' Cup Classic on dirt.

Volponi was bred by Amherst Stable, which consists of Johnson, his wife, Mary Kay, and their daughters Karen and Kathy, and owned in partnership by Amherst Stable and Spruce Pond Stable.

Volponi, though, is hardly the only stakes winner to come out of Johnson's barn. One of his favorites was Kiri's Clown, who won the very first race of the 1992 Saratoga meet under Jean Cruguet and returned three years later to end the worst slump of Johnson's career.

Johnson thought he was on the way to a successful summer in 1995 when he shipped Kiri's Clown to Rockingham Park and won the Grade 3 New Hampshire Sweepstakes Handicap on June 18th. But Johnson went the rest of the Belmont Park summer meet without a winner: zero-for-52. Then he lost his first 11 starts at Saratoga.

"This is the longest slump I've ever had," Johnson told Tim Wilkin of the Albany *Times Union*, July 28th, the day before he would saddle Kiri's Clown in the mile and a half, $250,000 Grade 1 Sword Dancer Handicap. "I remember I went three weeks at Arlington Park without a win in the late 1950s, but I've never had anything like this. When I was younger and had a slump, I would think it was the end of the world. When it got real bad, you'd want to commit suicide. But the reason I'm not winning is that I don't have horses that are capable of winning."

Kiri's Clown was. And the following afternoon, under a superb ride by Mike Luzzi, Kiri's Clown ended Johnson's ohfer by taking the Sword Dancer wire-to-wire. Hall of Fame trainer Billy Mott, whose King's Theatre finished third, congratulated Johnson afterwards and noted, "I'm sure he hasn't forgotten how to train racehorses."

You don't make it to the Hall of Fame if you do. Two years later, Johnson was inducted into the Hall of Fame. That's hardly his only recognition.

In 1983, Johnson was named the recipient of the New York Turf Writers Association's Red Smith "Good Guy" Award. In 1996, he was named "Good Guy" by the New York Press Photographers.

The truth is there aren't enough "Good Guy" awards in the world to honor Johnson, who lives every day simply and honorably while competing in the toughest racing community in the world.

"P. G. has helped so many people without telling anyone," trainer Tom Skiffington said. "Guys like me and John Hertler (an assistant to Johnson for 13 years before opening his own stable) and a whole pile of us. I trained a few horses P. G. sent me and he turned down $15,000 he had coming to him. He said, 'Just keep it.'"

When Johnson was inducted into the Hall of Fame in his third attempt in 1997—he'd been passed over in 1984 when Harry Trotsek was elected and in 1993 when Thomas J. Kelly was chosen—there was a letter to the editor in the Daily Racing Form from Barry D. Ross of Sharon, Massachusetts. In part it said,

"For me, his achievements pale in comparison to the mark he has made on the people with whom he has come into contact. As a college student in 1982 at the University of Kentucky, I had the good fortune to meet Mr. Johnson through his nephew, Jim McMullen, who like myself is now a horse trainer. I remember sitting in awe of Mr. Johnson as he talked about horses. His knowledge was so complete; he seemed to know of all facets of racing as well as breeding. He wasn't the least bit pompous, but he had a wealth of knowledge earned from working his way up from a one-horse stable to the top of his profession.

"As with any 18-year-old, I thought I had things pretty much figured out. After meeting Mr. Johnson, however, I realized I still had a long, long way to go. I remember thinking at the time that this man's knowledge would fill a wing in the Smithsonian, whereas mine wouldn't fill a small pamphlet.

"I worked hard, and about five years later took out my first trainer's license at Rockingham Park. The first person other than my own father to send me horses was Mr. Johnson. Since then, he has sent me several horses over the years, for himself as well as owners. He has always been great to work with, and quick to give you credit when the horses win. Truthfully, the reason many of the horses have won is because I had the good sense to follow his advice.

"As with many others in racing, I owe a lot to P. G. Johnson. The help he has given me over the years is something I'll not soon forget. As he was one of the first to help out a young trainer just starting out, let me be

one of the first to congratulate him on an
honor well deserved. The Hall is certainly a
better place with P. G. Johnson in it that it
was before. Other trainers' achievements
may equal his, but few can measure up to
the man himself."

The truth is, even getting to New York was an achievement for Johnson, who bought a horse named Song Master for
$75 at a 1942 auction in Chicago and won his first race with
him at Hawthorne Park in 1944.

Johnson journeyed to the Detroit Fair Grounds in the
mid-1940s to begin his career, then moved to Arlington Park in
1948, Florida in 1950 and New York to stay in 1962, though he
spent his summer of 1963 not at Saratoga, but at Laurel Park,
where he was the leading trainer. The only year Johnson raced
at Saratoga and did not win a race was in 1967.

Johnson has been the leading trainer at Belmont Park
four times, at Aqueduct three and at Saratoga once in 1983.

By then, Johnson had already made headlines, upsetting three-time Horse of the Year Forego with Quiet Little Table
in the 1977 Suburban Handicap, then winning 12 straight
stakes races he entered from 1978 through 1979.

In 1988, his three-year-old filly Maplejinsky won both
the Grade 2 Monmouth Oaks at Monmouth Park and the
Grade 1 Alabama at Saratoga.

Kiri's Clown gave Johnson another Grade 1 Saratoga
stakes victory in the 1995 Sword Dancer Invitational Handicap.
Johnson's other Saratoga stakes winners include A in
Sociology, Geraldine's Store and Naskra's Breeze.

But Johnson's lasting Saratoga legacy will be the streak.
"I never really planned on it, but it happened," he said. "I'm
going to try and keep it going. I'd love to continue it."

Winning the $750,000 Grade 1 Whitney Handicap with
Volponi in 2003 would have done so, but Volponi finished second by a length to favored Medaglia d'Oro, who had finished
a distant second to Volponi in the 2002 Breeders' Cup Classic.
Volponi then finished second again as the 4-5 favorite in the

$300,000 Grade 2 Saratoga Breeders' Cup to Puzzlement, trained by Johnson's long-time friend and Hall of Famer, Allen Jerkens. Johnson offered no excuses when he lost both races. "I think excuses cheapen your horse and your whole operation," Johnson said.

Volponi was on the way to a frustrating, but profitable, final year of racing before being retired to stud. In eight starts as a five-year-old in 2003, Volponi finished second five times and third twice. He didn't win a race, yet still made $438,256, upping his career earnings to nearly $3.2 million. His career ended with a disappointing performance in the 2003 Breeders' Cup Classic at Santa Anita, October 25th. He was fourth early, but tired to finish last in the field of 10, concluding his career with seven wins, 12 seconds and five thirds in 31 starts against the best competition available on dirt and turf.

The day before the Saratoga Breeders' Cup, Johnson had extended his Saratoga streak when Micmaceuse won the first race on August 15th under Jorge Chavez as the 7-5 favorite.

Asked about the streak, Johnson said, "If you point for it, you'll never do it. You just train your horses like everywhere else. It just happens."

For Johnson, it's been happening at least once at Saratoga for 36 years.

CHAPTER 14

An Unfunny Travers

A week before the 2003 Kentucky Derby, Jack Knowlton, the managing partner of Sackatoga Stable's Funny Cide, was on a panel of guests at the National Museum of Racing and Hall of Fame's annual pre-Derby seminar in Saratoga Springs. Knowlton was joined by three members of the media who were sharing their thoughts on the upcoming Run for the Roses. The National Museum of Racing holds the free seminars for the public annually before the Derby, before the Saratoga meet and before the Breeders' Cup.

Fans who attend—and the Hall of Fame room at the Museum is usually full with 150 to 200 people—receive a free Daily Racing Form and door prizes as a panel of handicappers/media types try to make sense of the immense handicapping challenge in front of them, be it the Derby, the Saratoga meet or the Breeders' Cup.

For the Derby, a bunch of prep races are shown and dissected. When Funny Cide's final pre-Derby race, the Wood Memorial at Aqueduct, was shown, the crowd went "ooooohh" when Funny Cide was passed by Kentucky Derby favorite Empire Maker in deep stretch and came on again to take another shot at him, losing by just half a length as Jerry Bailey wrapped up on Empire Maker.

Probably, most, if not all those in attendance at the Hall

of Fame, had already seen the Wood Memorial at least once, yet Funny Cide's determination elicited that collective sigh of approval from the crowd.

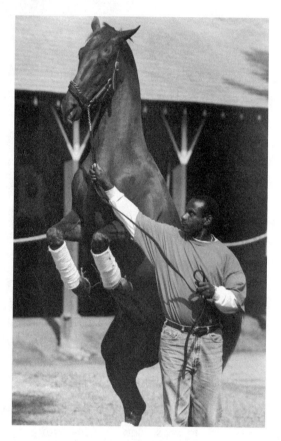

Funny Cide at Saratoga, 2003
(*Photo Courtesy of Barbara D. Livingston*)

Later, Knowlton diplomatically danced around the question of whether or not Funny Cide could reverse the decision in the Kentucky Derby, and added that no matter how Funny Cide performed on the first Saturday in May at Churchill Downs, the long term goal was clearly the Travers, the Mid-Summer Derby, at Saratoga, where Knowlton now works and lives.

When Funny Cide won the Kentucky Derby, becoming the first New York-bred to ever do so, he made celebrities out of his owners, a group of six high school friends from Sackets Harbor who had each thrown in $5,000 to form Sackatoga Stable and buy a Thoroughbred after a 1995 Memorial Day barbecue in Sackets Harbor on the shore of Lake Ontario. They designated Knowlton, who runs a health consulting firm in Saratoga Springs, as managing partner. The other original partners were Mark Phillips, Peter Phillips, Jon Constance, Harold Craig and Larry Reinhardt. David Mahan, Lou Titterton, Gus Williams and Eric Dattner became partners in the stable later.

Knowlton had previously owned Standardbreds in partnership with top driver Frank Coppola, Jr., and raced them across the street from Saratoga Race Course at Saratoga Harness, now known as Saratoga Gaming and Raceway. They called their stable The Breakfast Club because Knowlton, Coppola and other partners would invariably go out to breakfast Saturday mornings after their horses trained. "The arrangement I loved was that Frank was partners with all the horses," Knowlton said. "No matter what endeavor I'm in, I love it when you have a shared incentive. It's a win-win. You will pay more attention if you have some of your own money in."

The Breakfast Club did well with two warriors, Sunset Blue and Paulas Big Guy, Sunset Blue won the $40,000 final of the Pepsi Series at Saratoga, August 28, 1993, on the way to a career record of 33 wins, 33 seconds and 32 thirds and earnings of $270,356 from 209 starts in seven years. Paulas Big Guy earned $280,240 in his eight-year career from 49 wins, 52 seconds and 35 thirds in 259 starts. The Breakfast Club owned both horses for part of their careers.

But a labor dispute and horsemen's strike at Saratoga Harness sent Knowlton out of harness racing in 1994. So the following May, he talked his friends into buying a Thoroughbred.

Sackatoga Stable's first horse, a New York-bred named Sackets Six, cost $22,000 and won $111,730 under the guidance of trainer Tim Kelly before Sackatoga Stable sold him private-ly.

Four years later, Sackatoga Stable changed trainers, hiring Barclay Tagg. "I live two blocks from the racetrack, and I know a lot of people around the track," Knowlton explained. "Barclay had two stalls open and we had two horses."

Sackatoga Stable's first horse with Tagg, Bail Money, was purchased for $40,000 and earned $108,665 before being claimed for $62,500. "And the rest is history," Knowlton said.

That history started at Joe and Anne McMahohn's Saratoga Springs farm, McMahon of Saratoga Thoroughbreds, where Funny Cide was foaled in April 20, 2000. Funny Cide, a son of Distorted Humor out of Belle's Good Cide, a daughter of Slewacide, was purchased for $22,000, initially, at the Fasig-Tipton New York-Bred Preferred Yearling Sale at Saratoga by Tony Everard, who had taken care of Fourstardave at his Another Episode Farm in Ocala, Florida. The following spring, Sackatoga Stable bought Funny Cide from Everard for $75,000.

Funny Cide showed talent immediately on the racetrack, winning his debut by 14 3/4 lengths, September 8, 2002. He followed up with two victories in New York-bred stakes, the first by nine lengths, the second by a neck, to complete a perfect three-for-three two-year-old season. At three, he would compete exclusively in open company graded stakes. After finishing fifth in the Grade 3 Holy Bull Stakes from the extremely disadvantageous 13 post, Funny Cide was third in the Louisiana Derby to Peace Rules.

Funny Cide entered the Kentucky Derby off his gutsy second to Empire Maker in the Wood Memorial. Sackatoga Stable had so many people attending the Kentucky Derby that they rented a yellow school bus to accommodate them. That only added to the tale of 10 little guys striking it rich when Funny Cide, benefiting from a brilliant ride by Jose Santos, won the Run for the Roses by a length and three-quarters over Empire Maker, whose effectiveness might have been compromised by a bruised foot suffered earlier, possibly in the Wood Memorial. Peace Rules finished just a head behind Empire

Maker in third and only a head in front of late-running Atswhatimtalkinbout.

The Derby result was a surprise, but hardly shocking. Funny Cide had gone off the seventh choice in the wagering at 12-1 in the field of 16. Only Empire Maker (5-2), Peace Rules (6.30-to-1), Ten Most Wanted (6.60-to-1), Buddy Gil (7-1), Atswhatimtalkinbout (8-1) and Indian Express (10-1) were lower odds than Funny Cide.

But what happened next was bizarre. The Miami Herald ran a story the following week that Funny Cide's jockey, Jose Santos, might have used a buzzer in the race. But when hundreds, if not thousands of pictures of the Derby were blown up, it was clear that the so-called object in Santos hand was nothing but the shadow of the silks of Jerry Bailey, riding Empire Maker behind Funny Cide. The Kentucky Racing Commission investigated and quickly cleared Santos and Funny Cide. Coverage of the press conference announcing the Kentucky Racing Commission's decision reached mainstream TV, including CNN and MSNBC.

The class that Funny Cide's connections had shown after the Derby was re-enforced by the way they handled this gigantic screw-up. They took the high road and didn't lash out, though Santos and Sackatoga Stable sued the paper for $48 million a year later. When Funny Cide followed the Derby with the best race of his life, taking the Preakness Stakes by 9 3/4 lengths, just a quarter of a length off the largest margin in the long history of the second leg of the Triple Crown, Funny Cide and his owners on the yellow school bus were granted even more acclaim.

Funny Cide had moved within one victory of becoming the first Triple Crown winner since Affirmed in 1978. He would chase immortality in the mile and a half Belmont Stakes, where he would encounter not only Empire Maker, but also Ten Most Wanted, again. Empire Maker's trainer, Hall of Famer Bobby Frankel, and Ten Most Wanted's trainer, Wally Dollase, had decided to skip the Preakness to improve their chances in the longer Belmont Stakes. They would finish 1-2, Empire Maker dueling Funny Cide into defeat and then holding off Ten Most Wanted by three-quarters of a length in a miserable, unrelenting rain which had rendered the Belmont Park track a sloppy mess long before the horses walked on the track.

Again, Knowlton and crew showed tremendous class in handling the defeat; Knowlton just shrugging his shoulders seconds after Funny Cide finished third, missing the winner's share of the $1 million purse and Visa's $5 million bonus for completing the Triple Crown.

In its year-long review of sports in 2003, *USA Today*, December 24th, listed Funny Cide among the stories of "What's been so nice this year." *USA Today* noted, "High school buddies are sippin' on some brews and decide it would be fun to own a race horse. The result is a gelding who wins the Kentucky Derby. That leads to a couple more brews and the Preakness Stakes. Although there is no Triple Crown, it's one of the feel-good stories of the year."

After losing the Belmont Stakes, nothing would have felt better to Knowlton and his partners than having Funny Cide win the Travers Stakes at Saratoga. But there would be complications. In his first start after the Belmont, Funny Cide finished a listless third behind Peace Rules and Sky Mesa as the even money favorite in the $1 million Haskell Handicap at Monmouth Park. The next morning he was sick and there seemed to be little chance he would start in the Travers. That did not deter his fans from massing for a Funny Cide Day at Saratoga August 13th. Even a sudden rainstorm before his scheduled appearance in the paddock that morning did not keep his hundreds of fans from popping open umbrellas to greet him. But the 2003 Travers would belong to someone else.

After winning the 1997 Travers in the first Saratoga start for his trainer, Wally Dollase, Deputy Commander took the Grade 1 Super Derby before finishing second by six lengths to favored Skip Away in the 1997 Breeders' Cup Classic, beating both Behrens and Touch Gold in the process. They checked in seventh and last in the field of nine, respectively.

Dollase's only other Saratoga starter through 2002 was Crypto's Star, who finished third behind Awesome Again and

Tale of the Cat in the 1998 Whitney Handicap. Dollase third start at Saratoga would be in the 2003 Travers with Ten Most Wanted, a son of Deputy Commander.

They had much in common.

Deputy Commander was unraced at two; Ten Most Wanted had just one start at two, and that came late in the year when he finished second in his debut at Hollywood Park on November 29, 2002.

Both finished second in the Swaps Stakes before the Travers.

Both got a blinker change for the Travers—Deputy Commander shedding his and Ten Most Wanted having them restored.

Both won the Super Derby in their next start after the Travers, then lost in the Breeders' Cup Classic.

Aimee Dollase, Wally's daughter and assistant trainer, saw other similarities, as well. "Their heads are the same," she said before the 2003 Travers. "They have the same shoulder and the same personalities, but Ten Most Wanted is more powerful. He's put on weight and he's grown a lot since the Swaps."

Ten Most Wanted, whose dam Wanted Again was a daughter of 1990 Horse of the Year Criminal Type, was purchased for $145,000 as a two-year-old in the February 2002 Fasig-Tipton Sale at Calder Race Course in Florida by a partnership of Michael Jarvis, James Chisholm and Wally Dollase's Horizon Stable.

Ten Most Wanted had gone off at 14-1 in his debut, but when he returned to the races five weeks later, he was bet down to 3-5 and ran true to his odds, winning a maiden race by eight lengths.

The performance impressed Wally Dollase enough to move him up to restricted stakes company for his third career start, though Dollase could not have known how tough the field for the $81,000 Sham Stakes at Santa Anita would be, February 7, 2003. Man Among Men defeated Empire Maker by a length, while Ten Most Wanted pressed the early pace under Kent Desormeaux before fading to fourth, 8 1/2 lengths behind the winner. Desormeaux had ridden Ten Most Wanted in his first three starts but would be replaced by Hall of Famer Pat Day. Dollase made another change, removing the blinkers Ten Most Wanted had worn in all three starts.

Under Day, Ten Most Wanted finished a strong third by a length and a half to Ocean Terrace in the Grade 3 El Camino Real Derby at Golden Gate Fields. Dollase began thinking seriously about the Kentucky Derby, and Ten Most Wanted did nothing to discourage him by taking the Grade 2 Illinois Derby at Hawthorne in Chicago by four lengths as the 2-1 favorite, April 5th.

War Emblem had used the Illinois Derby as a springboard to the 2002 Kentucky Derby and won by four lengths. Dollase attempted to do the same with Ten Most Wanted, training him up to the Run for the Roses at Churchill Downs, May 3rd.

In the interim, two weeks before the Kentucky Derby, J. Paul Reddam purchased a 25 percent majority interest in Ten Most Wanted for a reported $1 million.

Though he drew a tough outside post, the 15, Ten Most Wanted would go off as the third choice in the 16-horse Derby at 6.60-to-1, but he suffered a brutal trip when he was off slow, bumped and checked. He finished ninth, 7 3/4 lengths behind Funny Cide.

Dollase decided he would point Ten Most Wanted to the Travers, and would use the Swaps as a stakes prep to get him there. Ten Most Wanted had injured his back in the Kentucky Derby and was treated by an equine chiropractor, "Ten Most Wanted's spine got knocked out of line," Dollase said. "The chiropractor really helped."

Sent off at 3-5 in the Swaps, Ten Most Wanted took the lead in deep stretch, then surrendered it to a dead-game colt, During, who re-took the lead and won by a head. Dollase would add blinkers to improve Ten Most Wanted's concentration.

Dollase shipped Ten Most Wanted to Saratoga three days before the 134th running of the $1 million Travers.

Who else would be in the Travers played out like a circus act, a poor one.

Both Empire Maker, who had finished second by a neck to Strong Hope as the 1-5 favorite in the $500,000 Jim Dandy Stakes at Saratoga, and Funny Cide, who was third in the Haskell at Monmouth Park the same afternoon, had been pointing to the Travers and would be entered in the Travers. But neither one would race.

Daily media briefings with Funny Cide's taciturn trainer, Tagg, played out like an episode of "General Hospital," with more attention given to Funny Cide's blood work than his work on the track at Clare Court, the tiny training track near Tagg's barn on the Saratoga backstretch.

Initially, after the Haskell, there seemed to be little hope of Funny Cide appearing in the Travers for a rematch with Empire Maker, who'd beaten Funny Cide in the Wood Memorial and Belmont Stakes but been beaten by him in the Kentucky Derby. Funny Cide spiked a temperature the morning after the Haskell, and seemed to be making slow progress until a week before the Travers. He recovered well enough to work, and went four furlongs in a quick :47.80 four days before the race, one his owners desperately wanted to make.

Suddenly, there was a chance that Funny Cide just might make the Travers, and his connections ponied up the $5,000 fee to enter the race. Then word leaked out that Empire Maker had been coughing. At the post position draw held three days before the race, Frankel downplayed Empire Maker's cough, but he also entered Peace Rules. Jerry Bailey was named to ride both Empire Maker and Peace Rules, which, in New York, meant one of them would scratch.

By Thursday evening, Frankel said that Empire Maker had mucous in his throat and wasn't eating well. Frankel scratched him the next morning.

When Tagg had Funny Cide scoped and also discovered mucous in his horse's throat, he scratched Funny Cide, too.

Both were out, leaving only six three-year-olds in: Peace Rules, Ten Most Wanted, Strong Hope, Sky Mesa and longshots Wild And Wicked and Congrats. Though he opened at 5-1, Peace Rules would be bet down to be the 2.30-to-1 favorite.

Sky Mesa had won his debut and the Grade 1 Hopeful Stakes at Saratoga in 2002, before being forced out of the Triple Crown chase by injuries. His second in the Haskell suggested to many that he was back at the top of his game, and he went off the 2.50-to-1 second choice.

Ten Most Wanted would go off as the 2.75-to-1 third choice.

Strong Hope, who had the meet's runaway leading trainer and jockey, Todd Pletcher and John Velazquez, would go off at 4.40-to-1 as he sought his sixth straight victory following a fourth in his career debut.

But Strong Hope, just like Peace Rules, was a speedster who had won five straight starts wire-to-wire. Peace Rules had raced on the lead in almost all his races. The speed duel they would generate in the Travers was not hard to handicap. The question was, if those two did hook up, who would benefit the most?

Class-wise, Ten Most Wanted and Sky Mesa towered over Congrats and Wild And Wicked. Congrats had closed well for third in the Jim Dandy, but never beaten top competition. Wild And Wicked had been three-for-three heading into the Haskell, but finished fourth by 10 lengths behind two horses he was facing again in the Travers, Peace Rules and Sky Mesa.

If Peace Rules and Strong Hope dueled themselves into defeat, then the Travers was either Ten Most Wanted's or Sky Mesa's. And that was exactly how the Travers played out.

Strong Hope, on the rail, and Peace Rules went at each other right from the start, racing head-to-head for the first mile of the mile and a quarter Travers, covering six furlongs in 1:09.98 and the mile in 1:35.46, both splits the second fastest in the Travers' lengthy history.

"If you have an option, you take it, but with these two horses, you don't have an option," said Bailey, who was riding Peace Rules for the first time. Velazquez concurred: "I tried my best to get him to settle, but as soon as Peace Rules got next to him, my horse got rank. There was nothing I could do."

Sitting behind the embattled pacesetters, Pat Day had little to do. Ten Most Wanted had settled comfortably in third on the rail. Right alongside was Edgar Prado on Sky Mesa, who had broken awkwardly but then been rushed into contention. As the field headed into the final turn, Sky Mesa couldn't keep up. Day eased Ten Most Wanted three-wide around Peace Rules and Strong Hope and he quickly collared the leaders and took control.

Strong Hope wilted at the top of the stretch, but Peace Rules fought on, keeping within a length of Ten Most Wanted until the final sixteenth. "He ran an incredible race," Bailey said.

Ten Most Wanted widened his lead to 4 1/2 lengths at the wire, while Peace Rules held on for second, 10 lengths in front of Strong Hope in third.

This time, Wally Dollase didn't have to tell his owners to wait before rushing to the winner's circle.

Dollase had become just the second trainer to condition both a Travers winner and the sire of a Travers winner. Bert Mullholland did so with Eight Thirty in 1939 and his son Lights Up in 1950.

Deputy Commander became the 12th Travers winner to sire another Travers winner.

A proud Dollase looked at Ten Most Wanted and said, "He looks so much like his sire. Both got it together mentally at this time of year."

Dollase just might have had something to do with it. He had journeyed from California to start three horses at Saratoga, all in Grade 1 stakes, and finished first, third and first. Two out of three ain't bad.

But when Funny Cide made his final 2003 start in the $4 million Breeders' Cup Classic at Santa Anita under Julie Krone—Jose Santos had committed to riding 2002 Breeders' Cup Classic winner Volponi—Funny Cide bore out badly on the first turn, carrying Ten Most Wanted extremely wide. Ten Most Wanted finished eighth to Pleasantly Perfect in the field of 10, a half length ahead of Funny Cide. The only horse Funny

Cide beat was, ironically, Volponi.

Yet Funny Cide had done enough to be voted Three-Year-Old Champion Colt over Empire Maker. The announcement came at the annual Eclipse Awards Dinner on January 26, 2004, in Florida, where Funny Cide had returned to the races 16 days earlier with an overpowering five-length allowance win at Gulfstream Park. Writing in the Blood-Horse Magazine, Scott Davis called Funny Cide "America's horse."

Ten Most Wanted, Pat Day up.
(Photo Courtesy of the Schenectady Daily Gazette)

CHAPTER 15

Another Four Bite the Dust

Hall of Fame trainer Bobby Frankel had a spectacular year in 2003, good enough to win his fourth consecutive Eclipse Award. That did not, however, preclude him from compiling a nasty, near month-long losing streak at Saratoga Race Course in 2003. When his Aldebaran won the Grade 1 Forego Handicap on August 31st, it was Frankel's first win since Medaglia D'Oro won the Grade 1 Whitney Handicap on August 2nd.

Saratoga's legacy as the "graveyard of champions" has stood the test of time, and the summer of 2003 was no different than summers of the previous 134 years, when high-profile horses that figure much the best go down to defeat in highly visible major stakes races.

Medaglia D'Oro and Aldebaran got the job done in their Grade 1 stakes, but three potential champions Frankel raced at Saratoga in 2003 went down in stunning defeat in the space of 19 days as odds-on favorites. Empire Maker would lose at 1-5 to Strong Hope by a neck in the Jim Dandy Stakes August 3rd in what would be Empire Maker's final career start. Spoken Fur would lose the Alabama Stakes at 4-5 to Barclay Tagg-trained Island Fashion 13 days later, costing Spoken Fur's connections a $2 million bonus. Then Wild Spirit would lose at 1-5 to Passing Shot, a longshot trained by Allen

Jerkens, in the Grade 1 Personal Ensign, by a nose on August 22nd.

Bobby Frankel, 2003
(Photo Courtesy of Barbara D. Livingston)

People had been predicting Empire Maker's greatness even before he finally stepped on the racetrack. He was a son of Kentucky Derby and Breeders' Cup Classic winner Unbridled out of the incredible mare Toussaud—a winner of just under $500,000 who produced $1.94 million earner Chester House, $894,168 winner Honest Lady and two other $400,000 earners, Decarchy and Chiseling. Empire Maker had been entered twice at Saratoga in his two-year-old season in 2002 without getting a chance to run. His long awaited debut came at Belmont Park, October 20th, when overcame the 12 post to win by 3 1/2 lengths as the 2-5 favorite.

Frankel upped the ante for Empire Maker's second start in the Grade 2 Remsen Stakes at Aqueduct, but Empire Maker finished third as the 7-5 favorite to Toccet.

Setting sights on finally getting his first Triple Crown victory, Frankel freshened Empire Maker and brought him back in a seemingly soft spot, the $81,000 Sham, a restricted stakes at Santa Anita, February 7th, for his three-year-old debut. Again sent off at 2-5, Empire Maker finished second by a length to Man Among Men.

Frankel added blinkers for Empire Maker's next start, the Florida Derby, and the colt finally delivered for Frankel and Jerry Bailey, the colt's only rider in his brief eight-race career. For the first time in his career, Empire Maker was not the favorite, going off at 2-1. But he dominated six rivals by 8 3/4 lengths. Suddenly, there was no more debate about who was the favorite for the 2003 Kentucky Derby. Bailey, in an uncharacteristic bold prediction, said that Empire Maker could become the first Triple Crown winner since Affirmed in 1978.

In the Grade 1 Wood Memorial at Aqueduct, his final start before the Kentucky Derby, Empire Maker surged past New York-bred Funny Cide in late stretch, but then the damnedest thing happened. While Bailey had Empire Maker wrapped up, Funny Cide took another run at him, losing by just half a length.

A bruised foot in the final week before the Kentucky Derby was probably the reason Empire Maker was allowed to go off the luke-warm favorite in the field of 16 at 5-2, instead of 3-2 or lower. This time, Funny Cide had more than enough to hold off Empire Maker after striking the lead. Funny Cide won the Derby by 1 3/4 lengths, becoming the first New York-bred to win the Run for the Roses.

Frankel decided to give Empire Maker a break and skip the Preakness Stakes, sending instead Empire Maker's stablemate, Peace Rules, who had finished just a head behind Empire Maker when third in the Derby. Funny Cide crushed Peace Rules, winning the Preakness by 9 3/4 lengths, the second largest margin in Preakness history. Funny Cide, not Empire Maker, would be going for the Triple Crown.

Empire Maker denied him. Under perfect handling by Bailey, Empire Maker wore down Funny Cide in a driving rainstorm, then held off Ten Most Wanted by three-quarters of a length to win the Belmont Stakes on a sloppy track. Funny Cide tired to third. Frankel had his elusive Triple Crown victory and Empire Maker's fans finally felt that the pecking order in the three-year-old division was finally the way it should have been—Empire Maker No. 1. After all, he had beaten Funny Cide in two of their three meetings.

While racing fans anxiously waited for their fourth meeting in the Travers Stakes, one which never happened with both horses scratching, Frankel chose the $500,000 Grade 2 Jim Dandy Stakes at Saratoga on August 3rd for his return. Funny Cide's connections opted for the $1 million Grade 1 Haskell Invitational half an hour later at Monmouth Park. Funny Cide would finish third.

Empire Maker had the softer assignment in the Jim Dandy. Of his five opponents, the only one with a realistic chance of upsetting him was Strong Hope, Eugene and Laura Melnyk's late developing son of Grand Slam trained by Todd Pletcher and ridden by John Velazquez. Both Pletcher and Velazquez were on their way to setting record totals in taking the Saratoga trainer and jockey championships in 2003.

Unraced at two, Strong Hope had finished a tiring fourth in his debut at Gulfstream Park, March 8th. He'd then reeled off four consecutive victories, all wire-to-wire. After winning his maiden and two allowance races, Strong Hope stepped up to contest the Grade 2 Dwyer Stakes at Belmont Park at a mile and a sixteenth. Strong Hope gutted out a neck decision over Jim Dandy opponent Nacheezmo and Sky Mesa. Strong Hope did it the only way he knew how, on the lead, and his winning time of 1:41.60 produced a sensational Beyer Speed Figure of 110.

In the Jim Dandy, Strong Hope was stretching out to a mile and an eighth for the first time and would have to deal with another front-runner, Bob Baffert-trained During, who had gamely re-taken the lead after being passed in deep stretch by Ten Most Wanted to win the Grade 2 Swaps Stakes by a head in his first race at a mile and an eighth.

During acted up badly before being loaded in the starting gate for the Jim Dandy and would go off at rather stunning odds of 23-1 under Pat Day from the three post. Only Congrats would be a bigger price at 30-1.

Strong Hope, breaking from the rail, went off at 6.70-to-1.

Empire Maker went off at 3-10 (1-5).

Strong Hope outgunned During for the early lead, and, once Day took hold of During, who faded to last, Velazquez tried to set a slow pace. Strong Hope got the quarter in :23.66 and the half in :47.17 before Tafaseel, a 9-1 shot under Richard Migliore, took a run at him with three furlongs of nine left to run. Strong Hope turned him back and opened a two-length lead at the top of the stretch as Velazquez waited for Empire Maker.

Fifth most of the way, Empire Maker moved up to second at the head of the stretch and went after Strong Hope. But Empire Maker ran strangely even as he advanced. Bailey hit him once left-handed and Empire Maker went sideways while still moving forward. One hundred yards from the wire, Strong Hope looked unbeatable, but Empire Maker made one final surge, coming up a neck short.

Afterwards, Frankel said Empire Maker "is a funny-running horse sometimes who seems to run in spots. I don't feel bad about losing this race."

Those who bet him sure did.

Frankel added that, "I think this race will set him up for the Travers," but Empire Maker never made it, getting sick two or three days before the race. He never raced again, retiring to stud with four wins, three seconds and a third in eight starts and earnings of $1,985,800.

Twelve days later, Frankel sent out his best three-year-old filly, Spoken Fur, in the 123rd running of the $750,000 Grade 1 Alabama Stakes at a mile and a quarter.

It's a funny thing about irony. It just happens.

For the first and only year in 2003, the New York Racing Association offered a $2 million bonus to any three-year-old filly who won the newly-configured Triple Tiara of Grade 1 stakes races, the Mother Goose and Coaching Club American Oaks at Belmont Park and the Alabama at Saratoga. Amerman Racing Stables Spoken Fur, trained by Frankel and ridden by Baily, had won the first two. Add in the $450,000 winner's share of the Alabama, and Spoken Fur could have picked up nearly $2.5 million.

And who would have a chance to deny Spoken Fur that gigantic payday? None other than Funny Cide's trainer, Barclay Tagg.

When Empire Maker beat Funny Cide in the Belmont Stakes, Funny Cide not only lost the winner's share of the $1 million purse, but also the $5 million bonus Visa offers to any Triple Crown winner.

Tagg didn't even have a top three-year-old filly in his barn that summer until fate intervened, delivering him a candidate for the Alabama, Jeffrey Nielsen's Everett Stables' Island Fashion. After a two month freshening, Island Fashion, who'd been a distant seventh to Alabama starter Bird Town in the Kentucky Oaks in her previous start, won the Grade 3 Delaware Oaks by 6 1/2 lengths July 19th.

Island Fashion had been trained by Nick Canani until Canani took an offer to become a private trainer for Michael Gill, the leading owner in the nation. When Canani accepted just after the Delaware Oaks, Island Fashion needed a new trainer to prepare her for her next start: the Alabama Stakes.

Nielsen does business with Tony Everard. So does Tagg. In fact, Tagg purchased Funny Cide for Sackatoga Stable from Everard for $75,000 in his two-year-old season. Nielsen suggested Canani send Island Fashion to Tagg, and that's exactly what Canani did. Tagg named Velazquez to ride Island Fashion in the Alabama

Still, Island Fashion was not the horse Spoken Fur had to beat. Bird Town was. Spoken Fur went off the 4-5 favorite with Bird Town the 8-5 second choice and Island Fashion 8-1.

But the Alabama was a one-horse race, giving Velazquez his fifth winner on the afternoon of August 16th. Velazquez let Island Fashion cruise in second behind front-running Awesome Humor, took over easily heading into the far turn and won by six lengths. Awesome Humor held second, a length in front of Spoken Fur. Bird Town was fifth in the six-horse field. "I wanted to creep up on the leaders, but I had no horse," Bailey said.

Frankel didn't say anything. He watched the Alabama from the racing secretary's office and vanished before reporters arrived.

Could Frankel and Bailey possibly lose six days later with Wild Spirit in the Grade 1 $400,000 Personal Ensign Handicap, named for the undefeated champion filly trained by Shug McGaughey? Frankel and Bailey looked invincible in a field of just five going a mile and a quarter with Wild Spirit.

After arriving from Chile, Wild Spirit had made two starts in the U.S. She won the Grade 2 Shuvee Handicap by 3 1/2 lengths under Javier Castellano at 10-1 then, with Bailey aboard, the Grade 2 Delaware Handicap by six lengths at 4-5, blowing away Take Charge Lady, one of the best older fillies in the country.

For the Personal Ensign Handicap, Frankel was adding the diuretic Lasix, a medication which can greatly improve performance when used for the first time.

If that wasn't enough going for Wild Spirit, she drew the rail, meaning Bailey could place her anywhere he desired. Theoretically.

Even though Wild Spirit would carry high weight of 122 pounds, only four rivals dared to take her on. Of the four, the one with the most credentials was Summer Colony, who had won the 2002 Personal Ensign Handicap by 4 1/2 lengths at 4-5. But she'd just been beaten 16 lengths by Wild Spirit in the Delaware Handicap. Miss Linda had been beaten 20 1/2 lengths when fourth in her last start, the Grade 1 Go for Wand Handicap, chasing Wild Spirit's stable-mate, Sightseek.

There were only two other fillies in the Personal Ensign and both were exiting the same allowance race. Passing Shot, trained by Hall of Famer Allen Jerkens and ridden by Jose Santos, had won that mile and an eighth race by three-quarters of a length over Golden Sonata.

Passing Shot, owned by Joseph Shields, Jr., had only raced in two restricted stakes on dirt, finishing fourth and fifth. Realistically, the only thing she had in her favor was the wizard who trained her, the Giant Killer: Allen Jerkens. Forever remembered for his historic upsets, including two of Secretariat with Onion in the 1973 Whitney Handicap at Saratoga and with Prove Out in the Woodward later that year at Belmont Park, Jerkens was enjoying an incredible year. He would finish 2003 with earnings topping $5.1 million to finish 14th nationally at the age of 74.

Even so, Passing Shot would go off the 11-1 third choice. Summer Colony was the second favorite at 6-1 and Wild Spirit went off at 1-5. More than $1 million was wagered on Wild Spirit to show by bridge-jumpers, bettors who load up on a heavy favorite to get the minimum $2.10 return. To reach that minimum, the track must cough up the difference, which is called a minus pool. This day, NYRA had to spend $184,505.50 to reward show bettors of Wild Spirit, who got a bigger thrill than they ever imagined.

Wild Spirit settled along the rail in third as Miss Linda led with Passing Shot stalking the pace. But as the position of the three leading fillies remained unchanged into the stretch, Bailey found himself trapped on the inside behind Miss Linda. Bailey waited and waited and finally found room on the inside of Miss Linda, who bore out a bit as she tired. Wild Spirit shot past everyone to take a clear lead, but Passing Shot had not given up. She kept coming, narrowing Wild Spirit's brief lead and then out-gaming her to the wire to win by a nose.

"I was very confident because I was riding for the Giant Killer," a jubilant Santos said afterwards.

When asked about the race, Frankel said, "This is not the right time for this."

It sure was for Jerkens. You can't pull off monumental upsets if you don't enter your horse against tough opponents in a stakes race. "It's always nice to run in a small field with a big purse," Jerkens said. "You have a chance to pick up something and you always have a chance you might win. All I wanted was to get her stakes placed if we could. Amazing, really amazing."

It was part of an amazing year for Jerkens. "It's always nice when it happens to you because when it goes the other way, you wonder what the hell you're doing wrong," Jerkens said.

Damned if he wasn't thinking that just two days later.

Jerkens found himself in unfamiliar territory when he tried making history by sending out the favorite in a stakes race, Bohemia Stable's Shine Again, in the $200,000 Grade 1 Saratoga's Ballerina Stakes. The six-year-old mare was trying to win the Ballerina for the third straight year. If she did, she would become just the third horse in Saratoga history to win a Grade 1 stakes three consecutive years. Discovery had done it by taking the Whitney Handicap in 1934, 1935 and 1936. Steeplechaser Happy Intellectual had won the New York Turf Writers Cup Handicap in 1976, 1977 and 1978.

Shine Again had been in the money in her last 13 starts and in 19 of her last 20. But her jockey in all of them, Jean-Luc Samyn, had been injured. Jerkens reached out to Santos again.

Shine Again went off the 5-2 favorite in the field of eight going seven furlongs. One of her opponents was You, who would finish seventh and later retire with nine wins, eight seconds and two thirds in 23 starts and more than $2.1 million in earnings.

You's Saratoga nemesis, Carson Hollow, who was named the 2002 New York-bred Horse of the Year, never made it back to Saratoga to race. She had a record of six wins and three seconds in 10 career starts—the lone poor effort in the Breeders' Cup Sprint as a three-year-old filly taking on older males—and earnings of just over half a million dollars when she became sick in the summer of 2003. She died from complications from colon surgery in Canada the day after the Ballerina.

Shine Again ran as hard as she possibly could and came up a nose short of the wire-to-wire winner of the 2003 Ballerina, Harmony Lodge, the longest shot in the field at 12.90-to-1 despite coming from Todd Pletcher's barn. Pletcher's main man, Velazquez, had chosen to ride Harmony Lodge's stable-mate, Smok'n Frolic, who went off the co-second choice at 7-2 and finished dead last. Richard Migliore was fortunate enough to pick up the mount on Harmony Lodge and he rode the five-year-old speedster masterfully from the outside post in the field of eight, keeping her together in the desperate final yards.

"I felt real confident when I let out a notch heading into the turn," Migliore said. "I had a lot of horse. I felt great about everything until about 70 yards out and the Giant Killer was looming large."

Pletcher, a class act, was asked how you beat the Giant Killer. "It's hard to do," Pletcher said. "Hats off to him. What a remarkable achievement to have a filly like that come within an inch of winning three Ballerinas in a row. That's hard stuff to do." Still, another stakes favorite at Saratoga, had gone down.

What Pletcher accomplished at Saratoga that summer, shattering Hall of Famer Sylvester Veitch's 1954 record of 21 winners for the meet with 35 was an amazing achievement itself. Pletcher got his 22nd winner on just the 15th day of the 36-day meet.

But that's another Saratoga tale.

My Own Saratoga Tale

Most people, when asked the question of, "What's the stupidest thing you've ever done in your life," have to think a minute or two.

Not me.
I answer right away.
I know just what to say.
It seems like yesterday.

WHEN I RODE AT SARATOGA

In a race.
Out of the starting gate!

What was I thinking? Wait a minute. I wasn't thinking. Kind of like my first marriage. Or my freshman year in college when they used pass/fail instead of grades. Seriously. As a freshman at Albany State in 1971-1972, there were no grades. Nada.

That's a brilliant idea. Take several hundred teenagers over the drinking age of 18 and away from home for the first time in their lives, put them in co-ed dorms, and remove every incentive they have to attend classes, let alone study. Yeah, that'll work.

And that still wasn't as dumb as what I did on a Sunday afternoon in 1980, after I graduated from Albany State with a

political science degree, which, by the way, has had a lot of rel-
evance in my life as a sports writer. As opposed to my three
years of studying French in high school. After waiting more
than 30 years, I was presented an opportunity to utilize my
French in a real-life situation. In 2003, trying to arrange a tele-
phone interview with the legendary French trainer Andre
Fabre, I was confronted on the phone by a woman who spoke
no English. None. I quickly resorted to my extensive French
vocabulary from high school and came up with, "Je m'appelle
Guillaume," which may mean "My name is William." Or "I like
potatoes." Either way, the conversation didn't get very far. I
could have added the only other French sentence I remembered, "Paul est a la bibliotheque," which I think is, "Paul is at
the library," but I didn't think it would add much to the conversation. I called back. Actually, I had tried using my high
school French once in Montreal to order a beer. They brought
me a toaster.

YOU CAN RIDE AT SARATOGA!

The invitation seemed innocuous enough when it
arrived at the sports department of the *Times Union* newspaper
in Albany in the summer of 1980:

> Join us for a media race at Open House
> at Saratoga the Sunday before the meet
> opens. With FREE T-shirts!

Do you have any idea what the word "FREE" means to
the media? It's a sacred word, kind of like "mother" or
"money." The only term holier than "FREE" is when the word
"FOOD" is attached to it. Writers have been known to rise from
their graves at a whiff of a FREE lunch.

FREE T-shirts wasn't as inviting as FREE FOOD, but it
was still enticing, especially since I only owned about seven
thousand of them. You can never have too many T-shirts,
right?

Let's see. What did I have to do to get this FREE T-
shirt? Ride a horse? But I'd never ridden a horse before. I bet-

ter call and find out the details. No sweat. They said they might use donkeys for the race. No big deal. Have a great time.

Hmmm. Was anybody else going from the *Times Union*? My sports editor, Eddie Palladino, was. Eddie had just returned from back surgery, was a tad overweight and had never ridden a horse either. He was in. Well, if he's in, I'm in. We'll go as an entry, 1 and 1A.

That decision was made on a Friday morning two days before the race. Friday afternoon, there was a phone call about the Media Race at Open House. They couldn't get donkeys. So, instead, they're going to use trail horses. No big deal. They run together as a pack.

At this precise moment, my brain screamed, "HELLLPPPPP!!!" but my mouth said, "Okay."

By the time I hung up the phone, I cleverly deduced that I needed a crash course in riding horses. I called a nearby riding stable and sped there for a half-hour lesson. When I told the friendly riding instructor that I was going to be in a race at Saratoga in two days, she looked at me as if I was from Mars. But, after she stopped laughing, she said she would do what she could to prevent my impending doom and give me a lesson.

Most of the lesson consisted of my futile attempts to get on my horse, Chester.

I felt like Neil Armstrong when I finally made it onto the saddle. I wanted to plant a flag.

"The first thing we're going to do is walk," the instructor said.

Wrong. The first thing we're going to do is watch Chester eat grass.

"You can't let him do that," the instructor implored. "You have to teach him who's in charge."

I said, "Look-it, he knows who's in charge; I know who's in charge, and you know who's in charge."

Chester eventually got tired of grazing and we did walk a bit before the lesson ended. My instructor walked away shaking her head, which I interpreted as not a good sign.

All of Saturday and Sunday morning was spent in pure panic. What had I been thinking? How could I possibly to learn to ride a horse in half an hour? It had to take at least an hour.

Now I'm heading to Open House, which annually draws up to 15,000 people. At least there would be a lot of witnesses.

This was the first year of the Media Race, and so many people had entered that they had to split the race into three divisions. Eddie and I landed in the second division, which at least gave us the opportunity to see the first. All three divisions would race a sixteenth of a mile right in front of the grandstand.

But first, before we got our FREE T-shirt, we had to register, and sign, what's this? A waiver? Why are we signing a waiver? Brilliantly, I decided if I signed my name as "Bill" instead of my legal first name "Guillaume," rather "William," that my wife could sue following my demise.

Eddie and I walked out onto the track to watch the first division. Why was there a starting gate at the sixteenth pole? And why were the horses in the first division being loaded into the starting gate?

ARE THEY NUUTS? Are they completely out of their minds?   Professional   jockeys   riding   experienced Thoroughbreds had been hurt and killed in starting gate accidents.

The horses were loaded. The starting gate opened, and out came the horses in the first division. Only one person fell, without hurting herself, fortunately, but another contestant who had ridden horses before couldn't pull her mount up. The horse did a complete lap of the track. That's a mile and an eighth. Finally, they came to a stop near the finish line.

If that wasn't frightening enough, we then learned that the organizers hadn't been able to get enough horses for three divisions, so they were using the same ones three times.

That was comforting.

Eddie and I weighed out options: punk out in front of more than 10,000 people and never hear the end of it from our friends in the media, or go ahead and tempt fate.

The author (second from right)
beats his editor (far right), Eddie Palladino
(*Photo Courtesy of Skip Dickstein*)

In that moment of decision, I thought of what was really important. The FREE T-shirt. Hell, no, I'm not giving that back. There's a principal involved here.

We got a leg up in the paddock and walked our horses onto the track. I had no idea what I was doing, but the horses were following one another toward the starting gate. I had the No. 4 stall; Eddie the No. 2.

As my horse contemplated entering the starting gate, I realized how incredibly narrow the stall was. I didn't think there was enough room for my horse and my legs, which I thought would be ripped off. I waited in dread. The gates opened. I still don't remember the first couple of seconds, but I remember the first word out of my mouth:

"WHOOOOAAAA!!!!"

We flew through a sixteenth of a mile—okay, it wasn't

as fast as Secretariat, it just felt that way—and, miraculously, my horse decided to stop after the finish line. I had finished fifth in a field of seven or fourth in a field of six. But the best news was that my life wasn't finished. Eddie, who was fifth or sixth, was also okay, although the horse he rode had to wear a truss for the rest of his life.

I dismounted with the stupidest grin on my face. I had survived. And I had learned a life lesson from this, a very important one:

If You Have to Sign a Waiver, It Might Not
Be a Good Idea.

Unless, of course, there's a FREE T-shirt. The aches in my body from riding a horse went away. Eventually. So did my first wife. And the Media Race did not survive. But I've still got that T-shirt. Did I mention that it was FREE?

Index

A Phenomenon 64-65, 75
Ace Personality 45-46
Adlibber 40-41, 51-52
Admiral Bayard 149
Affairwithpeaches 131
Affirmed 25-26, 28-31, 33-35, 117, 123
Affirmed Success 131-132
Aldebaran 169
Allumeuse 3, 91-94, 96, 98-99, 103, 105-106
Alydar 25-35, 52, 123
Alysheba 121
Ambehaving 7
Amello, Tom 83
Amending 116
Ancient Title 19
Angle Light 19
Anka Germania 123
Anonymous Prince 51
Antley, Chris 70
Arcangues 12
Arcaro, Eddie 57
Armstrong, Neil 181
Arranger 56
Atswhatimtalkinbout 161
Attfield, Roger 125
Audience 11-12

Awesome Again 127, 130-131, 162
Awesome Humor 175

Babae 144-145
Baeza, Braulio 8, 12, 18, 60
Baffert, Bob 172
Bailey, Jerry 4-5, 57, 93, 95-96, 98, 101, 127, 130-133, 139-140, 143-147, 157, 165, 167, 171-172, 174-175
Baltazar, Chuck 12
Barrera, Laz 25-26, 28-31, 35, 61, 110
Barrett, Janet 42
Batteur 39
BC Sal 73
Behrens 5, 127, 132-134, 162
Believe My Curves 71
Belle's Good Cide 160
Belmonte, Eddie 17-18, 56
Big Band Show 116, 118
Big If 38
Bird Town 174
Blazing Sword 131
Bold Arian 77
Bold Forbes 61-62

Bold Igloo 45-46, 48
Bold Ruler 14
Bomze, Richard 75-80, 86, 88
Bond, Jim 4-5, 124-127, 130, 133-135
Bond, Tina Marie 134
Bookstein, Joyce Hellman 9, 11, 22
Bookstein, Sanford 9, 18, 21, 23
Borden, Dave 45
Bowers, Virginia B. 9
Brenner, Aaron 105
Broadway Joan 77-78
Buddy Gill 161
Bundle of Money 116
Burch, Elliott 16
Burke, Jerry 95
Burning Roma 151-152

Came Home 121
Campfire 138
Campo, Johnny 11, 45, 49, 51
Canani, Nick 174
Cannonade 58
Cannonero II 13
Captain Bodgit 122
Carr, Dennis 86
Carr de Naskra 125
Carson City 139
Carson Hollow 145-147, 178
Cassidy, Brian 42, 45, 49, 52
Cassidy, George 1, 41-46, 48-50, 52
Cassidy, Mars 41-42
Cassidy, Marshall 41-42, 47, 52, 98, 110-111
Cassidy, Wendell 42
Cassie's Birthday 51

Cauthen, Steve 12, 25-26, 28, 33, 45, 62-63
Chain Bracelet 39
Chapman, James 138
Chavez, Jorge 156
Chehana 93
Chenery, Christopher 14
Chenery, Penny 14
Cherokee Run 139
Chester 181
Chester House 170
Chief's Crown 67
Chieftan 7, 21
Chiseling 170
Chisholm 163
Cicada 14
Cigar 126
Citation 13
City Zip 138-141
Clabber Girl 111-112
Clancy, Joe 119
Clancy, Sean 3, 115-119
Clemente, Christoph 144
Clifton,Jr. William 126-127, 133
Climb The Heights 67
Cocks, Burley 92
Codex 61
Cohen, Ruth 9
Columbus Circle 110
Combs, II, Brownell 64
Compliance 77-78
Congaree 139
Congrats 166, 173
Conoby, Tom 17
Constance, Jon 159
Contradance 67
Coppola, Jr., Frank 159
Cordero, Jr., Angel 4, 17-18, 26, 52, 55-72, 81-82, 93, 100-111
Cordero, Marjorie Clayton 71

Coronoado's Quest 134
Courtneys Doll 77
Coyote Dancer 66
Crafty Admiral 25
Craig, Harold 159
Crème De La Fete 62
Criminal Type 163
Cruguet, Jean 67, 93, 103, 152
Cryptoclearance 150
Cryptocloser 131
Crypto's Star 162
Cunningham, Tom 1, 11, 50
Cusano, Mark 18
Cute As A Button 33

Danzig 92
Darby Creek Road 28
Dattner, Eric 159
Davis, Robbie 65, 82, 95-96,
  110-112
Davis, Scott 168
Dawn's Fancy 93-94, 96, 99,
  100, 103
Day, Pat 70, 93, 121, 131, 164,
  167, 173
Decarchy 170
Dehere 28, 138
DeMare, Carol 9, 22
Deputy Commander 5, 122-
  123, 128, 131-133, 162-163
Deputy Minister 123
Desert Law 39
Desormeaux, Kent 164
Discorama 39
Discovery 177
Distorted Humor 160
D. J.'s Nitecap 45, 51
Dollase, Aimee 123, 163
Dollase, Carrie 123

Dollase, Cindy 123, 133
Dollase, Craig 123
Dollase, Michelle 123
Dollase, Wally 4-5, 122-124,
  132-134, 162-165, 167
Douglas, Mae 21
Dream Path 7
Dumb Donna 77
Dupps, Lucas 100-102
During 164, 172-173
Durkin, Tom 86-87, 146
Dust the Plate 8
Dutrow, Jr., Richard 146

Easy Goer 126
Edgewater 93
Editor's Note 127
Edmondson, Dr. Alan 21
Eight Thirty 167
Elocutionist 61
Empire Maker 159-161, 163-
  165, 168-173
Erin's Word 40
Estrada, Jose 80
Evening Attire 139-141
Everard, Tony 78, 88, 160, 174
Excellent Tipper 86
Exceller 117
Exclusive Native 25

Fabersham 70
Fasta Dancer 93-95, 102
Feliciano, Paul 16-17
Fell, Jeff 32, 45-46
Ferrara, Sal 95, 101-102, 104
Festivity 93-94, 96, 99-100, 103
Fitzsimmons, Sonny Jim 41
Foolish Pleasure 28

Forego 19, 155
Fourstardave 4, 73-89
Fourstars Allstar 80-81
Frankel, Bobby 19, 39, 143, 145,
   161, 165, 169-176
Frazier, Joe 94
Free House 122-124
Fried, Jr., Albert 131
Funny Cide 4, 69, 73, 157-162,
   164-165, 167-168, 171-172, 174

Gallant Fox 43
Gamely 39
Gann, Edmund A. 145
Garramone, Anthony 45
Gator Ray 56
Genuine Risk 61
Gersowitz, Bob 7, 17
Gill, Michael 174
Gleaming Light 13
Go for Wand 75
Goldberg, Hank 87
Golden Sonata 176
Gonzalez, Bernie 26
Gonzalez, Mike 45
Good Behaving 12-13
Goodman, Lenny 12
Goodman, Mary 139
Grand Slam 172
Grant, Arnold 44
Great Neck 63-64
Grecian Flight 112
Grening, Dave 124
Gulch 59
Gullo, Tom 11

Hamilton, Dick 95, 100
Happy Intellectual 177

Harmony Lodge 178
Hasty Matelda 14
Hellman, Edith Marx 9-10, 13,
   22-23
Hellman, Harry 9
Hellman, Neil 4, 7-13, 21-23
Hellman, Nettie 9
Hello 122
Hennessy, Joe 82
Hernandez, Ruben 1, 37-38, 41,
   47, 62
Hertler, John 153
Hettinger, John 38, 51- 52
Hickey, Noel 124
Highfalutin 59
Hofmans, David 131
Honest Pleasure 61
Hurler 117-118

Image Of Class 93
I'm Your Boy 59
Indian Express 161
Island Fashion 169, 174-175

J. O. Tobin 32
Jacobson, Buddy 11
Jaipur 143
Jarvis, Michael 163
Jatski 34
Jenney, Marshall 92
Jerkens, Allen 33, 45, 139, 156,
   169-170, 176-177
Joan's Dancer 78
Jocoy, Jock 20
John Henry 66, 121
Johnson, Karen 151
Johnson, Kathy 152
Johnson, Mary Kay 152

Johnson, Phil "P. G." 4, 45, 92, 149-156
Jolley, LeRoy 112
Jones, Aaron 20
Jones, Marie 20
Judger 58

Kelley, Robert "Tony" 95, 101-102, 104
Kelly, Tim 160
Kelly, Tom 28, 153
Key to the Mint 116
King, Joe 110, 129
King's Theatre 153
Kiri's Clown 152-153, 155
Kling, Faye 83
Kling, Nick 83
Knowlton, Jack 157-159, 162
Krone, Julie 70-71, 166-167
Kronfeld, Eric N. 91

LaCroix, Joseph W. 7
Lady Hardwick 60
Lady Marinat 67
Lady's Secret 91
Lamb Chop 39
Laughing Bill 13
Laughing Bridge 22
Laurin, Lucien 15, 19
Layden, Tim 101-102, 104
L'Carriere 125-127
Legacy Of Strength 93
Lemhi Gold 20
Lights Up 167
Linda's Chief 3-4, 7-8, 13, 18-22
Lines of Power 63
Lone Mountain 116
Lovato, Jr., Frank 45-47, 51-52

Louis Quatorze 126-127
Lucky Touch 100
Lukas, D. Wayne 61, 111, 132, 139
Lure 87- 88
Luzzi, Mike 153

MacBeth, Don 65, 67
Macho Uno 139-141
Mac's Fighter 82
Madagascar 93
Mahan, David 159
Majesty's Prince 66
Maloney, Jim 38-41, 47-49
Man Among Men 171
Man o' War 3
Maple, Eddie 26, 28, 45, 58, 60, 62-63, 66-67
Maplejinsky 155
Marder, Keith 112
Markey, Admiral Gene 27
Markey, Mrs. 27, 30
Marlin 122
Maxzene 106
McCarron, Chris 4, 58, 82, 121-122, 124, 128, 130-132, 135
McGaughey, Shug 139, 175
McHargue, Darrell 45
McKenzie Bridge 62
McKeon, Gerard 48-49, 110-111
McLaughlin, Dick 95, 101-102, 104, 110
McMahon, Anne 160
McMahon, Joe 160
McMullen, Jim 154
McNair, Janice 131
McNair, Robert 131
Melnyk. Eugene 172
Melnyk, Laura 172

Meyocks, Terry 130
Micmaceuse 156
Miesque 82
Migliore, Carmela 73
Migliore, Richard 62-63, 73, 75, 83, 85-87, 89, 151, 173, 178
Miller, Chip 115-117
Millerick, Buster 123
Miss Linda 175-176
Montoya, Darryl 81
Mott, Billy 153
Mourjane 75, 93, 106
Move It Now 1, 3, 37-38, 40, 45-46, 48, 50-51
Mrs. Penny 92
Ms. Eloise 111
Mugatea 65
Mullholland, Bert 167
My Thief 123

Nacheezmo 172
Nakatani, Corey 122, 132
Naskra's Breeze 45-46, 48
Nasty and Bold 33
Native Courier 63-64
Native Dancer 138
Nerud, John 63
Nielsen, Jeffrey 174
Nijinsky's Gold 86
Nolan, Howard 12, 21
Northstar Dancer 14, 17-18
Novel Notion 63

O'Brien, Keith 78-79, 81-82, 84, 88-89
O'Brien, Leo 71, 74, 76-84, 88, 90
O'Brien, Michael 77

O'Brien, Vincent 81
On-and-On 26
Once And For All 68
Onion 3, 176
Orlando, Don 128-130
Orlando, Michael 128
Orseno, Joe 139
Our Mims 27
Our Native 20

Palace Panthe 106
Palladino, Eddie 181-183
Paneto, Wigberto 83, 96, 98, 103
Paradise Career 87-88
Pass Catcher 13
Passing Shot 169, 176
Passing Thunder 94, 99-100
Paula's Big Guy 159
Payson, Virginia Kraft 125
Peace Rules 160, 162, 165-167, 171
Peck, Brian 112
Penna, Jr., Angel 64
Perlsweig, Dan 10-11
Persian Mews 106
Persian Tiara 66
Peters, John 20
Petigrow, Charles 51
Phillips, Mark 159
Phillips, Peter 159
Phipps, Ogden 14
Phipps, Ogden "Dinny" 48-50, 104
Piermont, Dave 78
Pincay, Jr., Laffit 19, 25-26, 33-35, 58, 60
Pitts, Clinton 118
Pleasantly Perfect 168
Pletcher, Todd 166, 172, 178

Point Given 141, 151
Prado, Edgar 139, 167
Prenuptial 116
Pricci, John 94, 98-99, 103
Prom Knight 150
Prove Out 176
Puzzlement 156

Quebec 16
Quiet Little Table 155
Quintessential 45-46, 48-49, 51-52

Raffie's Majesty 134
Raise a Native 26
Rasmussen, Leon 20
Reddam, J. Paul 164
Regal and Royal 28
Reina Blanca 144
Reinhardt, Larry 159
Relaxing 62
Riboletta 20
Rice, Linda 138-140
Ridan 143
Riddle, Samuel 43
Right Approach 52
Right On Louie 45-46
Riley, Victor 21
Riva Ridge 15
Roberto 116
Roberto's Grace 3, 115-119
Roberto's Social 93
Rock, Damien 88
Rogues Walk 71
Romero, Randy 80, 93, 112
Roosevelt, Jr., Franklin 63
Rosen, Theodore 13
Rose's Cantina 111-112

Ross, Barry D. 153
Royal Manner 45-46
Rudder, Anne 125
Rudder, Donald 125
Ruffian 22, 113
Run Dusty Run 34

Sackets Six 160
Sailer Go Home 14
Saint Verre 139-141
Samyn, Jean-Luc 45-46, 177
Sande, Earl 43
Santos, Jose 56, 68-70, 93, 97-98, 103, 112, 138, 140-141, 144, 160-161, 167, 176-177
Scorpion 139, 141
Scotti, Al 8, 11-13, 17-19
Screenland 37, 40, 45-46, 48, 51
Seabiscuit 43
Seattle Meteor 112- 113
Seattle Slew 32, 117
Secretariat 3, 14-19, 28, 176
Sensitive Prince 33
Shadowmar 65
Shake Shake Shake 33-34
Sham 19
Sheppard, Jonathan 116
Shields, Jr., Joseph 176
Shine Again 177-178
Sightseek 175
Silver Charm 122-124
Sir Harry Lewis 150
Skiffington, Tom 91
Skiffington, Jr., Tom 70, 91-93, 97-98, 103-104, 106-107, 153
Skip Away 162, 166
Sky Mesa 162, 167, 172
Slewacide 160
Slew City Slew 103

Smith, Mike 70, 84
Smith, Red 2
Smok'n Frolic 178
Snow Dance 144
Somethingroyal 1-15
Song Master 155
Spoken Fur 169, 173-175
Sports Reporter 77
Spring, Virginia Spain 10
Star de Naskra 29
Steinlen 82-83
Stephens, Woody 58, 92
Step Nicely 18-19
Stop the Music 18-19
Strickland, Dick 129
Stronach, Frank 131
Strong Hope 166-167, 169, 172-
    173
Sugar Dottie 40
Sullivan, Charles 101
Summer Colony 175-176
Summer Guest 16
Sunset Blue 159
Sweet Tooth 26
Syntonic 93-96, 99-100, 102-103

T P Louie 140
Tabor, Michael 139
Tafaseel 173
Tagg, Barclay 160, 165, 169, 174
Take Charge Lady 175
Tale of the Cat 163
Tantivy 62
Taormina, Sal 76
Tates Creek 144-145
Temperence Hill 61
Ten Most Wanted 161-168, 172
The Bride 14
Three Martinis 39

Threewitt, Noble 123
Tiffany Lass 20
Tiltalating 67
Tilt Up 28
Timeless Moment 38
Titterton, Lou 159
Tiznow 121
Torraca, Joseph 105
Touch Gold 123-124, 127, 131,
    134, 162
Trevose 14, 17
Tri Jet 32
Turcotte, Gae 16
Turcotte, Ron 13, 15-18, 60
Turner, Billy 45
Twice the Vice 122
Twin Spires 131-132

Unbridled 170
Upset 3
Ussery, Bobby 149
Utah Pine 93-95

Valdez, Steve 20-21
Valley Victory 77
Van Lindt, John 50
Vasquez, Jacinto 60-61
Veitch, John 25, 27, 29-35
Veitch, Sylvester 27, 178
Velasquez, Jorge 19, 25, 29-30,
    34-35, 45, 68, 93, 110
Velazquez, John 71-72, 145-147,
    166-167, 172-174, 178
Victory Gallop 134
Vindaloo 67
Vittorioso 65
Volponi 69, 149-152, 155-156,
    167-168

von Wiesenthal, Bonnie 39-40,
  46-51
von Wiesenthal, Peter 39, 49
Voodoo Dancer 144-145
Voss, Tom 115, 118

Wakefield Tower 77
Waldman, Leo 40
War Admiral 43
Warfare 38
Warfingers 38
Watters, Sidney 93
Way Of The Barron 70
Whiteley, Frank 77, 92
Wicked Will 63-64
Wild And Wicked 166
Wild Cataract 85
Wild Spirit 169, 175-176

Wilkin, Tim 68-69, 152
Williams, Gus 159
Williams, Mordechai 15
Will's Way 126-127, 134
Wings of Grace 116
Winter Affair 71
Without Words 45-46, 48, 51-52
Wittles Lane 45-46
Wolfson, Louis 25
Wolfson, Patrice 25, 33, 35
Won't Tell You 25

Ycaza, Manny 60, 70, 72
Yonaguska 138-141
You 145-146, 178

Zyglewicz, Dave 94, 105